A Balanced Approach to Beginning Reading Instruction

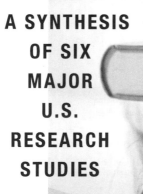

A SYNTHESIS OF SIX MAJOR U.S. RESEARCH STUDIES

JOHN EDWIN COWEN
Fairleigh Dickinson University
Teaneck, New Jersey, USA

INTERNATIONAL
Reading Association
800 BARKSDALE ROAD, PO BOX 8139
NEWARK, DE 19714-8139, USA
www.reading.org

The International Reading Association attempts, through its publications, to provide a forum for a wide spectrum of opinions on reading. This policy permits divergent viewpoints without implying the endorsement of the Association.

Director of Publications   Joan M. Irwin
Editorial Director, Books and Special Projects   Matthew W. Baker
Production Editor   Shannon Benner
Permissions Editor   Janet S. Parrack
Acquisitions and Communications Coordinator   Corinne M. Mooney
Associate Editor, Books and Special Projects   Sara J. Murphy
Assistant Editor   Charlene M. Nichols
Administrative Assistant   Michele Jester
Senior Editorial Assistant   Tyanna L. Collins
Production Department Manager   Iona Sauscermen
Supervisor, Electronic Publishing   Anette Schütz
Senior Electronic Publishing Specialist   Cheryl J. Strum
Electronic Publishing Specialist   R. Lynn Harrison
Proofreader   Elizabeth C. Hunt

Project Editor   Janet S. Parrack

Cover Design   Linda Steere

Web addresses in this book were correct as of the publication date but may have become inactive or otherwise modified since that time. If you notice a deactivated or changed Web address, please e-mail books@reading.org with the words "Website Update" in the subject line. In your message, specify the Web link, the book title, and the page number on which the link appears.

Library of Congress Cataloging-in-Publication Data
Cowen, John E.
    A balanced approach to beginning reading instruction : a synthesis of six major U.S. research studies / John Edwin Cowen.
        p. cm.
Includes bibliographical references and index.
    ISBN 0-87207-515-X (alk. paper)
    1. Reading (Early childhood)—United States. 2. Literacy—United States. I. Title.
    LB1139.5.R43C69 2003
    372.4--dc21
                                                                    2003001831

Dedicated to my supportive and encouraging family—

Jay, Jill, and Juliet

CONTENTS

PREFACE   vii

CHAPTER 1   1
Toward a Definition of a Balanced Approach to Reading Instruction

CHAPTER 2   11
The Cooperative Research Program in First-Grade Reading Instruction (the First-Grade Studies)

CHAPTER 3   22
Learning to Read: The Great Debate

CHAPTER 4   30
Becoming a Nation of Readers:
The Report of the Commission on Reading

CHAPTER 5   39
Beginning to Read:
Thinking and Learning About Print

CHAPTER 6   52
Preventing Reading Difficulties in Young Children

CHAPTER 7   61
Report of the National Reading Panel:
Teaching Children to Read: An Evidence-Based Assessment
of the Scientific Research Literature on Reading and Its
Implications for Reading Instruction

SUMMARY   79

APPENDIX A   83
Activities for Applying Literacy Concepts

APPENDIX B   87
Questions for Cooperative Discussion Groups

REFERENCES   89

INDEX   93

PREFACE

Teachers have agonized over the following basic questions since the teaching of reading to young children began: Should I teach phonics? If so, where and when do I begin? How much phonics instruction is necessary? What methods or approaches should I use? What texts, materials, and technology are most useful? In turn, these same questions are asked with the anticipation that, once understood and implemented, all recipient children will become successful readers; and if not, tried and true remedies will likely resolve any difficulties that arise.

Preservice, new, and veteran teachers are still asking these questions and with the same positive expectations, which to most casual observers, including parents, business leaders, and politicians, would seem to have very simple, direct, and universal responses. Unfortunately, these anticipated outcomes have not been realized so readily. Instead, there has been no consensus among groups of classroom teachers, reading specialists, university professors, and even some literacy researchers with regard to how to best teach children to read. Consequently, pedagogical confusion has continued to exist and has been greatly exacerbated by debates referred to as "the reading wars" (Snow, Burns, & Griffin, 1998, p. v). Historically, there has been a lack of agreement by the reading profession with regard to reading acquisition: namely, the use of phonics versus whole language—meaning-based—approaches. In the wake of these reading wars, struggling readers are rendered helpless, or, as Snow and colleagues (1998) state, "the focus of attention has shifted from the researchers' theories and data back to the teacher, alone in her classroom with a heterogeneous group of children, all awaiting their passports to literacy" (p. vi).

As one might imagine, these pedagogical differences are not a result of professional irresponsibility or a lack of need to use the best of all possible solutions to end illiteracy. Rather, there is a historical disagreement on how to attack the complex issues of teaching reading. In part, some in the reading field fear that a regimen of teaching "the code" (i.e., using knowledge of the "alphabetic principle" and phonics to decode unfamiliar words) directly relegates young children to using worksheets and enduring skill drills that will dull their senses and abrogate their interest in reading authentic literature forever. Another issue is that although teachers and researchers agree that meeting the needs of all children who are diverse socioeconomically, culturally, and also in ability is an admirable goal, it is difficult to attain because of the complexity of teaching a language that is among the world's most difficult to learn. This difficulty is due mainly to the English language's historically irregular spelling system (orthography) (e.g., *knight* or *night*), which makes it nearly impossible for at-risk readers to identify—no less, learn to decode—words from sound-symbol relationships required by the alphabetic system on which the written language is based. Owing to this linguistic complexity, we must never allow it to be used as an excuse for teachers or students to adopt an attitude of learned helplessness.

Finally, all interested parties within and outside the educational community need to know how difficult it is to learn to read, and to understand that there are no simplistic answers or easy solutions to these nagging and major problems (Snow, Burns, & Griffin, 1998). Nevertheless, there is hope that these problems can be resolved once teachers' knowledge base and their ability to put research findings into practice converge. Surely, the literacy research of the past 30 years can empower us all to overcome linguistic hurdles and to prevent reading difficulties in our youngest children.

The three major purposes of this book are (1) to summarize and review six influential U.S. studies of reading research about beginning reading (see Table 1); (2) to show how these studies support a balanced approach to beginning reading instruction; and (3) to make these research findings and conclusions more accessible and reader friendly to classroom teachers, preservice teachers, related language arts and literacy educators, professors, and interested community stakeholders, which will result in more informed decision making in teaching reading to young children. The information in this book should provide guidance in answering those difficult questions posed at the beginning of this preface and, perhaps, even empower classroom teachers to engage in their own research with their own struggling

TABLE 1
Authors, sponsors, and advisors for six U.S. reading research syntheses

Title	Year	Authorship	Sponsor(s)	Advisory Group
The Cooperative Research Program in First-Grade Reading Instruction	1967	Guy L. Bond Robert Dykstra	U.S. Department of Health, Education, and Welfare, Office of Education, under the provisions of the Cooperative Research Program	The Coordinating Center of the Cooperative Research Program in First-Grade Reading Instruction; Bond and Dykstra coordinated 27 project directors.
Learning to Read: The Great Debate	1967	Jeanne S. Chall	Carnegie Corporation	No formal advisory group but significant reviews by several scholars
Becoming a Nation of Readers: The Report of the Commission on Reading	1985	Richard C. Anderson Efrieda H. Hiebert Judith A. Scott Ian A.G. Wilkinson	National Academy of Education (NAE), National Institute of Education, Center for the Study of Reading	NAE Commission on Reading: Richard C. Anderson Isabel Beck Jere Brophy Jeanne S. Chall Robert Glaser Lenore Ringler David Rumelhart Dorothy Strickland Sue Talbot Monte Penney
Beginning to Read: Thinking and Learning About Print	1990	Marilyn J. Adams	Office of Educational Research and Improvement, U.S. Department of Education	Ira Aaron Jeanne S. Chall Bernice Cullinan Linnea Ehri Philip Gough Dorothy Strickland Robert Ruddell
Preventing Reading Difficulties in Young Children	1998	The Committee on the Prevention of Reading Difficulties in Young Children Catherine Snow, Susan Burns, and Peg Griffin (Eds.)	Office of Special Education Programs, Office of Educational Research and Improvement, National Institute on Child Health and Human Development	Catherine Snow, chair Marilyn Jager Adams Barbara T. Bowman Barbara Foorman Dorothy Fowler Claude N. Goldenberg Edward J. Kameenui William Labov Richard K. Olson Annemarie Sullivan Palincsar Charles A. Perfetti

(continued)

Table 1 (continued)

Authors, sponsors, and advisors for six national reading research syntheses

Title	Year	Authorship	Sponsor(s)	Advisory Group
				Hollis S. Scarborough
				Sally E. Shaywitz
				Keith Stanovich
				Dorothy S. Strickland
				Sam Stringfield
				Elizabeth Sulzby
Report of the National Reading Panel: Teaching Children to Read: An Evidence-Based Assessment of the Scientific Research Literature on Reading and Its Implications for Reading Instruction	2000	Members of the National Reading Panel, with Donald N. Langenberg, chair. NRP Subgroup chairs serving as editors: *Alphabetics* Linnea Ehri *Comprehension* Michael L. Kamil *Fluency* S.J. Samuels Timothy Shanahan *Methodology* Timothy Shanahan Sally E. Shaywitz *Teacher Education* Gloria Corerro Michael L. Kamil *Technology/Next Steps* Michael L. Kamil	1997 U.S. Congress request to the National Institute of Child Health and Human Development (NICHD), Secretary of Education charged a National Reading Panel (14 members)	Members of the NRP (14 members) Donald N. Langenberg, chair Gloria Correro Linnea Ehri Gwenette Ferguson Norma Garza Michael L. Kamil Cora Bagley Marrett S.J. Samuels Timothy Shanahan Sally E. Shaywitz Thomas Trabasso Joanna Williams Dale Willows Joanne Yatvin

Adpated from P.D. Pearson (1999), p. 236.

beginning readers to solve some of the elusive and unresolved literacy issues that still bemuse researchers today.

As illustrated in the following chapters, each of the six research studies—conducted on a national scale and supported by U.S. federal agencies, institutes, and associations—lends credibility to ending the reading wars in favor of developing a "common ground" (Adams, 1990a; Anderson, Hiebert, Scott, & Wilkinson, 1985; Bond & Dykstra, 1967; Chall, 1967; National Institute of Child Health and Human Development, 2000; Snow, Burns, & Griffin, 1998). Once teachers—

novices and veterans, alike—begin to apply research judiciously to their practices, they will forge energies capable of ensuring successful reading attainment for their students through an integrated, balanced approach to reading instruction. This approach, described in detail in chapter 1, is one that is orchestrated in a well-crafted manner. It is not a "cookie-cutter" or "one-size-fits-all" design nor is it a predetermined recipe for literacy, measuring out 2 cups of this, 2 cups of that, and 2 cups of the other—with a "pinch thrown in for the pot." It is important, therefore, to state here that a balanced approach to reading instruction is necessarily built on children's strengths, and that *balance* refers to the assessed present and future language developmental needs of children. In other words, to be an effective practitioner in a balanced reading program, the classroom teacher must know the literacy strengths and weaknesses of every child under his or her domain, and from this vantage point, the teacher can become an effective "balanced literacy" provider. Consequently, the balanced literacy teacher helps create young readers, writers, thinkers, and communicators—once they are given the opportunity to develop—within an integrated, comprehensive, and seamless learning environment that teaches the mysterious unraveling of words for the purpose of making and conveying meaning through exciting literacy adventures.

Building Consensus Through Research

There will always be naysayers; nevertheless, it is encouraging to read a body of historical literacy research—more than 30 years' worth—conducted by the most respected reading professionals in the field, which reaches consensus on several debated issues. In the following chapters are summaries of these six major studies that show how similar the findings and recommendations are, while at the same time depicting how each of these reports provides converging evidence that suggests the need for a balanced approach. According to Pearson (1999), "all of the reports can be construed as supporting a balanced approach to literacy" (p. 244).

The selected studies are presented chronologically by year of publication (see Table 1). There are those who might argue that Chall's

(1967) *Learning to Read: The Great Debate* should be presented before Bond and Dykstra's (1967) *The Cooperative Research Program in First-Grade Reading Instruction* (the First-Grade Studies), because Chall began collecting data as early as 1959 and some of her preliminary research results actually appeared earlier than Bond and Dykstra's completed study. However, the First-Grade Studies have established quite a legacy. The studies have significantly influenced the direction of reading instruction and even Chall's own studies, as she admits: "How many confirmations of the First-Grade Studies do we need before we put its findings to use?" (1999, p. 10).

The rationale and criteria for selecting the six research studies for this book are as follows:

- Each study provides a U.S. national synthesis of current knowledge about beginning reading instruction.
- Each study contains elements of a balanced approach to reading instruction that can be construed as a recurring theme throughout.
- Each study is supported by a nationally recognized and authoritative council, academy, or research body.
- Each study is important not only to reading professionals, but influences policymakers and the general public.
- Each study is readily recognized by reading professionals, educators, and policymakers and, therefore, provides credibility and authority in establishing future resources for literacy improvement programs and materials.
- The studies as a whole provide a high degree of converging evidence that can be disseminated nationwide to build support for developing future exemplary literacy programs that will help meet diverse students' needs.
- The studies as a whole can serve as a retrospective screening process for analyzing future beginning literacy research investigations that promote balanced literacy.

The synthesis of the research on balanced reading instruction for beginning readers can serve as a catalyst to provide greater dialogue and opportunity for putting an end to the senseless reading wars that have distracted and even disrupted our youngest children from learning to read successfully. The synthesis provided here should also provide a clearer perspective of current knowledge about beginning reading research, particularly with regard to findings on the importance of phonics instruction in creating a balanced approach to reading instruction. Albeit, the summaries should be read with a certain awareness; that is, most of these studies reported are based primarily on scientific, quantitative, empirical research restricted mostly to controlled groups and laboratory settings in contrast to qualitative, action research conducted in classrooms where teacher-student interactions and behaviors can be taken into account, are analyzed, and from which conclusions are drawn and reported. According to Dorothy S. Strickland (1998), past president of the International Reading Association and an advisory member to three of the studies, "Much of the research cited...is grounded in experimental studies in which children's demonstration of performance is based on the results of standardized tests" (p. 48). With this caveat in mind, the reader must determine how much agreement, or at least convergence, can be attributed to the last 30 years of literacy research and if these historical sources are persuasive enough to give classroom teachers reason to seek common ground and end the controversy. After thoroughly reading and rereading each of the studies, I believe there is enough converging evidence to convince reading professionals to use a common ground approach. By seeking balance we will be able to establish common goals and essential elements of a balanced reading program, supported by research—and common sense—so that we can put into practice what has been proven to work. It is possible today to help our youngest readers learn how to read more successfully than ever before, particularly by taking advantage of what so many years of conclusive evidence from research assures us about the effectiveness of a balanced approach to reading instruction.

Overview of the Chapters

Chapter 1 defines what a balanced reading approach to beginning reading instruction is and what it is not.

Chapter 2 discusses Bond and Dykstra's (1967) First-Grade Studies, the first U.S. national studies on beginning reading instruction. The studies concluded that a strong phonics emphasis is more valuable than a basal-driven, meaning or sight-word approach to early reading instruction, while emphasizing other important language factors that require more than just the code to support balanced reading. Its experimental research approach compares various reading methodologies. The study is often praised for the evolution of emergent literacy research, staff development programs in literacy, and the recurring theme that there is "no one best approach" to reading instruction. The published results of the studies first appeared in *Reading Research Quarterly* in 1967. Printed again in 1997 to commemorate its 30th anniversary, the studies were accompanied by several reflective essays written by notable researchers of literacy, making them accessible to a new generation of readers.

Chapter 3 compares the conclusions from Chall's (1967) *Learning to Read: The Great Debate* to those of the First-Grade Studies. In contrast to Bond and Dykstra (1967), however, Chall reviewed relevant research from 1900 to 1965, finding converging evidence that phonics is an essential approach to successful reading acquisition. Chall found that the emphasis on a systematic code approach is more effective than using a basal reading series, which focuses on reading for meaning. She also concluded that learning the alphabetic code, combined with good teaching and the use of appropriate level reading materials, leads to successful reading achievement.

Chapter 4 shows how Anderson, Hiebert, Scott, and Wilkinson's (1985) *Becoming a Nation of Readers: The Report of the Commission on Reading* (BNR), using a methods-comparison-research design, supports the two previously mentioned reports. This study provided insight into the need for providing more attention to students' comprehension as part of a balanced reading approach, including more time for students to read meaningful text and children's quality literature. BNR points to the reciprocal impact that writing has in influencing reading and how learning conventional spelling and phonics contributes to better reading achievement. BNR is one of the first reports to indicate that phonics instruction should be taught simply and early, ending by second grade for most children. BNR also is the first study to emphasize helping at-risk children learn how to read, a consequence, perhaps, of the U.S. National Commission on Excellence in Education's (1983) highly publicized and controversial document *A Nation at Risk: The Imperative for Educational Reform.*

In chapter 5, Adams's (1990a) *Beginning to Read: Thinking and Learning About Print*, about basic processes and instructional practices in word and letter identification in early reading, builds on several new bodies of research, including phonemic awareness and invented spelling, orthographic knowledge, the importance of concepts about print, and the processes involved in learning to read and write. Although this study does not indicate that one reading approach is better than another, it does stress the value of teaching phonograms using a phonics approach with onset and rime. The study also confirms that letter-recognition facility and phonemic awareness are necessary early code requisites for beginning reading success.

In chapter 6, Snow, Burns, and Griffin's (1998) *Preventing Reading Difficulties in Young Children* (PRD) provides a synthesis of the current available research on the best practices in teaching reading to children in preschool through grade 3. The intended purpose of this study was to help prevent reading problems from arising, while at the same time to identify methods of instruction that might work best for at-risk children and for other children demonstrating problems learning how to read. The findings and conclusions, however, indicate that there are few approaches that are more effective with high-risk children readers compared to low-risk readers. In fact, PRD research concludes that excellent instruction is the best intervention for all children, including, perhaps, the need for much more intensive support with high-risk readers.

In chapter 7, the National Institute of Child Health and Human Development's (NICHD) (2000) *Report of the National Reading Panel: Teaching Children to Read*, known for its evidence-based assessment of the scientific research literature, was the most recent U.S. national report published at the time I synthesized the research on beginning reading. The report, conducted at the behest of the U.S. Congress in 1997, was published in two volumes: a summary report and a more comprehensive Reports of the Subgroups. It is the second volume that presents the findings and recommendations for classroom practice and is, therefore, synthesized for practical purposes. The National Reading Panel, consisting of 14 members, was assigned to analyze the findings designated by the National Reading Council's report (Snow, Burns, & Griffin, 1998) as central to learning to read: alphabetics, fluency, and comprehension. After public hearings were conducted, however, the Panel included two additional topics—teacher education and computer technology—relating to reading instruction.

Following the chapters, the Summary outlines major points made throughout the book and provides a brief commentary on the need for future research and on research that is currently underway.

In the appendixes are dialogues and applications of concept activities that provide opportunities for preservice and inservice teachers and other interested readers to engage in cooperative discussion groups and related simulated experiences.

Few classroom teachers to whom I have spoken have had the inclination or expertise to read in their entirety the six studies synthesized in this book. Therefore, I hope that my analysis and review simplifies the research and enables preservice and classroom teachers and other educators to understand and benefit from this information, and empowers them to improve reading instruction so that beginning readers learn how to read.

Toward a Definition of a Balanced Approach to Reading Instruction

Following years of disagreement and debate about how to teach reading, it appears that a consensus is possible if only phonics advocates and whole language enthusiasts find a common ground. Many have thought that the debate would never end; however, there are signs that the controversy is beginning to abate. For instance, fewer articles with a stance either for or against phonics or whole language are being published in reading journals. According to Gaffney and Anderson (2000), whole language was at its peak between 1986 and 1996 but began waning in 1996. One U.S. national survey found that 63% of elementary teachers believed that phonics should be taught directly, and that 89% believed that skills instruction should be combined with literature and language-rich activities (NICHD, 2000). This kind of teacher support for phonics would have been unheard of only a short time ago.

Since 1990 when Marilyn Jager Adams's *Beginning to Read: Thinking and Learning About Print* appeared, many notable educators have written about and endorsed the efficacy of teaching phonics, reading, writing, and spelling in the classroom (i.e., Marie M. Clay, 1993; Patricia M. Cunningham, 2000; Irene Fountas, 1996; Gay Sue Pinnell, 1998; Regie Routman, 1994; and Dorothy Strickland, 1998). And, it has become apparent that more and more elementary school teachers and reading specialists are giving the concept of balanced reading a chance and are willing to reach agreement in finding a common ground where whole language and phonics can coexist. For example, Vail (1991) shows that structure (skills) and texture (language) can be combined with the principles of good teaching, namely, using authentic literature while teaching phonics systematically and painlessly.

The six research studies discussed in this book also have contributed to our understanding of how a balanced approach to reading instruction works in a more dynamic and fluid way (see Table 1, pp. ix–x). Susan B. Neuman (2001), former director of the Center for the Improvement of Early Reading Achievement (CIERA) and current U.S. Assistant Secretary for Elementary and Secondary Education, writes, "We encourage all teachers to explore the research, open their minds to changes in their instructional practice, and take up the challenge of helping all children become successful readers" (p. iii). This call for teachers and other reading professionals to look to research as a way of finding this balance is an important, positive trend. However, even the term *balanced reading* has become a recent cause for discussion, if not confusion. A number of articles and books describing and defining balanced reading approaches, analyzed by Freppon and Dahl (1998), explain that teachers must realize that balanced instruction is more complex than the term conveys. In fact, effective balanced instruction requires a very comprehensive, integrated approach, demanding that teachers know a great deal about literacy research related to emergent literacy, assessment-based instruction, phonological and phonemic awareness, the alphabetic principle, phonics and word study, selecting appropriate leveled readers, reader response, writing process, and constructivist learning. In the balanced reading classroom, all of these essentials must be addressed, and the teacher also must meet the demands of a multicultural society that requires him or her to be knowledgeable about teaching English language learners to read.

Balance, therefore, is a complex issue and cannot be resolved with simple solutions such as measuring out equal doses of phonics and whole language, as some have misinterpreted the term to mean. Instead, balanced reading needs to be described exponentially. As Pressley (2000) suggests, instruction aimed at promoting comprehension skills should be "multicomponential" (p. 557). Multicomponential elements should include the development of decoding skills, sight words and rich vocabulary development, specific comprehension skills, and reading within a sociocultural context. Other multicomponential instructional areas necessary for developing balanced reading include extensive authentic reading and writing; use of semantic and syntactic contextual cues; self-monitoring and self-regulation; and practice in reading with fluency, speed, and accuracy.

Freppon and Dahl (1998) address the nagging problem of interpreting balanced reading instruction, using the former extreme models of whole language versus phonics instruction. Some harsh critics of balanced reading instruction, such as Louisa Cook Moats (2000), would have teachers believe that *balance* is used only to advance whole language, wrongly asserting that, "whole language about how reading is learned has been contradicted by scientific investigations" (p. 5). Moats also distorts so-called scientific research findings by reporting, "reading science is clear: young children need instruction in systematic, synthetic phonics in which they are taught sound-symbol correspondences singly, directly, and explicitly." In fact, the six studies presented here insist that there is no one approach that has been deemed to be the best method; therefore, the "synthetic phonics" approach is not regarded by scientific research to be the best or only method for teaching phonics. Researchers now generally agree that early reading instruction does require a "systematic" approach to phonics, albeit an analogy form of phonics that utilizes onset and rime or spelling patterns and has proven to be an equally effective, systematic phonics approach. For instance, Pressley (2002) cites the use of spelling patterns—a decoding-by-analogy approach to word identification—which is supported by scientifically based research as having produced "roughly comparable gains in decoding" (p. 164). The reading community must be wary of the misinformation and distortion of research findings similar to the statement made by Moats (2000) that only a synthetic approach to teaching phonics is known to be effective. Adams (1990a) not only cites the effective use of an onset and rime or phonogrammatic approach to phonics, but she also recommends its use without reservation. Pressley (2002) cites the National Reading Panel's conclusions that contradict Moats's claims:

> Even though Chall (1967) had concluded that synthetic phonics (i.e., instruction teaching students explicitly to convert letters into sounds and blend the sounds) is more effective than other forms of systematic phonics instruction, *the Panel* [author's emphasis] reported no statistically significant advantage for synthetic phonics instruction over other phonics approaches. (p. 335)

Unfortunately, as Pressley (2002) discovered when he read more than 20 recent books about balanced reading instruction, few books are really about balance at all; instead, most are written with a specific bias: to state why reading should be more skills based or more whole language based. I fear that some influential literacy experts will continue to waste their energy, as well as confuse their readers, by delimiting the meaning of the term *balance* instead of researching how to best employ a truly balanced reading program that teaches all children how to read. Dixie Lee Spiegel (1998) takes a humorous, ironic view of the all-or-nothing approach espoused by Moats and her counterparts who reject a phonics–skills approach to reading. Spiegel believes that a truly balanced approach can work because it is not restricted to a misguided search for the "silver bullet" (p. 114), which has failed in the past and will surely fail again if not checked. She provides three characteristics of a balanced approach to reading instruction that should form the foundation on which all beginning reading programs are developed. The approach

- is built on research,
- views teachers as informed decision makers and therefore is flexible, and
- is built on a comprehensive view of literacy. (p. 117)

According to Spiegel, this "comprehensive view of literacy is inclusive, not exclusive" (p. 118) and consists of at least six major components:

1. Literacy involves both reading and writing.
2. Reading is not just word identification, but word identification is part of reading.
3. Readers must be able to take different stances in reading: aesthetic and efferent.
4. Writers must be able to express meaningful ideas clearly.
5. Writing is not just grammar, spelling, and punctuation, but those are all part of effective writing.
6. A comprehensive program develops life-long readers and writers. (p. 117)

In a *New York Times* article, Richard Rothstein (2001) reports that G. Reid Lyon, chief reading researcher at the National Institutes of

Health (NIH), stated that the term *balance* "is only an excuse to ignore phonics research" (p. B7), therefore, calling instead for a "comprehensive approach" to reading. Snow, Burns, and Griffin (1998) similarly state that they prefer the term *integration* to *balance* because an integrated approach more clearly defines the seamless requirements of a comprehensive, coherent approach to beginning reading instruction. Instead, we might equate the term *balance* with the term *moderation,* used by the ancient Greeks to describe their philosophy of living. It seems that this view is echoed by Dorothy Strickland (1998) in her statement, "Avoiding instructional extremes is at the heart of providing a balanced program of reading instruction" (p. 52). To avoid future debates about which approach to literacy to use, we must not advocate either-or ultimatums. We must avoid instructional extremes, or we will not be able to move forward in implementing literacy instruction that integrates skills in a balanced, comprehensive, thoughtful, and caring way. Another recently debated question is How much should teachers teach directly and explicitly? Alexander and Jetton (2000) state that the answer to this question lies between the extremes and depends on the reader's level of comfort relative to the content or the strategies undertaken.

Educators would be better served by providing a balanced approach to reading instruction that is more reflective of New Zealand's literacy instruction, which combines several approaches and materials, as well as procedures, to create "more balanced programmes"(Holdaway, 1979, p. 142) in their schools. Holdaway (1979) presents five elements of a balanced program that have existed in New Zealand for more than two decades:

1. Using Guided Reading: Using the basic series (individualized leveled texts), monitoring progress (i.e., Clay's running records), and decoding and reading for meaning.

2. Using Language Experience Procedures: Linking language and experience to spoken and written language.

3. Using Individualized Reading Procedures: Conferencing of teacher and child for reading, skill development, and self-selecting books.

4. Using Shared-Book Experience: Using Big Books in group experience procedures.

5. Using Developmental Activities: Using children's literature, story, verse, song, and chants.

Fountas and Pinnell (1996) outline many of these same elements, including components such as reading aloud, shared reading, independent reading, modeled and shared writing, interactive writing, and independent writing. According to Debra Johnson (1999), teachers identify within the guided-reading, small-group session, and they teach specific assessed-skill areas including phonemic awareness, phonics, concepts of print, comprehension, and other interventions that are based on developmental stages and related benchmarks within the balanced reading curriculum. In this way, beginning reading is taught in a balanced, integrated manner; phonics and meaning are taught seamlessly and as needed, not because of a preconceived notion and not because one ideology is promoted over another.

McIntyre and Pressley (as cited in Freppon & Dahl, 1998), in concert with Vygotsky (1934/1978) and Clay (1991), recommend the following key practices that lead to balanced instruction based on children's cultural and background information, as well as their interests, strengths, and needs:

- using an assessment-to-instruction model of teaching;
- respecting children's backgrounds, language, interests, and abilities;
- using information about the learners' culture, values, knowledge, and interests to plan instruction;
- teaching strategies and skills explicitly using a whole-part-whole approach that returns the learner to meaningful whole text; and
- providing planned, systematic instruction on needed strategies (McIntyre & Pressley, as cited in Freppon & Dahl, 1998).

Through observation of children, and assessment-based teaching, teachers develop a clearer understanding of their children's reading ability, informing themselves about what, how, and when to intervene. For instance, knowledge of Clay's (cited in Adams, 1998) three cueing systems—semantics (meaning), structure (syntax), and graphophonics (visual)—helps teachers know which cues and patterns children are employing as they read. Teaching phonemic awareness and phonics to children whose assessed needs indicate that this type of instruction is required is important for their future reading success. Also, based on children's assessed needs, teachers who take running records are empowered to see what children need and are more likely to teach the code, sometimes employing skills in a contextual reading approach and sometimes in the form of direct instruction. The more empowered teachers are, the more knowledgeable they become about research and instructional alternatives and the more likely they are to use a balanced approach to reading instruction.

Despite an apparent move toward reconciliation among disparate factions of reading professionals by endorsing balance in their reading programs, other reading professionals fear that the term *balanced reading instruction*, as yet, has not been defined clearly. As a result, school districts may begin buying "balanced reading kits" and end up in just as bad a situation as they were in the past. In a session on balanced reading at the 1999 International Reading Association Annual Convention in San Diego, Jerome Harste admonished more than a thousand teachers, saying, "We need knowledgeable professionals in the classroom. Instead, we are back in the business of buying programs [rather than] teaching kids how to read.... Teacher-proof materials just don't work!" A number of such foreboding predictions have been echoed by Freppon and Dahl (1998); Pearson (1999); Reutzel (1999); Spiegel (1998); and Wharton-McDonald, Pressley, Rankin, Mistsretta, Yokoi, and Ettenberger (1997).

D. Ray Reutzel (1999) states that balanced reading "is defined anew without attention to 'our reading past'" (p. 322). He also is concerned that the perception many have is that phonics is equal to whole language, and, therefore, instruction should be a 50-50 proposition; but that is not what is needed. This author has similar concerns having been witness to too many pendulums swinging from one side of the skills ledger to the other. Consequently, it is recommended that this is the moment to be cautious and to reconsider, to review the research closely, and to make decisions judiciously. In a study I conducted on balanced reading (Cowen, 2001), a group of 20 prekindergarten through third-grade teachers who had been immersed in the literature and in some recent studies related to balanced reading began grappling with the question What should be the essential elements of a balanced reading program? Cassidy and Wenrich (1998) exhort that we must not forget our reading past and that a successful program must be a combination or blend of whole language and phonics instruction. In response, my inquiry with the teachers culminated in 15 essential elements for developing a truly balanced reading program. Of course, this list should not be viewed as complete nor is it intended as a model to be adopted. Instead, the following elements are presented only as a representative list forged from a strong philosophical belief system that enabled one particular group of teachers to develop their own thoughtful, integrated, comprehensive approach to balanced reading (Cowen, in press):

We believe that a balanced reading program should provide

1. authentic, real literature, including nursery rhymes, fairy tales, and poems that provide students with opportunities to read and enjoy a variety of genres (fiction, nonfiction, and themes), including a rich assortment of multicultural resources;

2. a very comprehensive writing-process program that engages students in daily writing, peer editing, and publishing activities;

3. an integrated language arts and phonics skills-development approach that requires skills to be taught from the context of real literature as well as from student writing;

4. attention to the three cueing systems—semantics, syntactics, and graphophonics—to give students the required blend of skills, enabling them to read texts meaningfully and with understanding;

5. metacognitive, self-monitoring, fix-up, and scaffolding strategies to support student word recognition and reading comprehension;

6. opportunities to develop learning strategies to use in new situations and to acquire new information to develop higher order thinking skills;

7. ongoing assessment for continuous progress that engages students at the independent or instructional reading level and avoids reading materials at their frustration reading level;

8. oral storytelling, dictation, and other listening activities, including phonological and phonemic awareness development at the primary level;

9. an interdisciplinary content area reading approach, stressing the use of a wide variety of trade books as well as textbooks;

10. shared reading, guided reading, independent reading, and one-on-one instruction, particularly for struggling readers;

11. time commitment to on-task reading, writing, and related language arts activities;

12. reading/learning centers for exploration and discovery in all areas of the language arts and for managing individual and differentiated instruction;

13. opportunities for developing and maintaining a language rich environment;

14. a supportive, nurturing classroom that meets the diverse needs of students and that also promotes listening, speaking, reading, writing, and viewing as joyful experiences; and

15. promotion of ongoing family involvement in children's literacy development.

This list is indicative of a professional group of elementary teachers who are open to change and willing to incorporate a comprehensive and integrated approach to literacy for the benefit of all children. It is evident that this approach is comprehensive and integrated and could be woven into most teachers' definition of balance. Within these 15 elements are phonemic awareness, phonics, reading literature for understanding, and writing as a process to engage children in joyful expression and communication. It is also apparent that this group of teachers put aside differences to find a common ground, and that their choice of essential elements will help them to address the various strengths and needs of their students to help them become better readers, better writers, and better communicators.

A Balanced Approach to Beginning Reading Instruction should provide easier access to the research for teachers and other individuals who are interested in refining their own definition of balanced reading. I recently have been empowered to write a personal definition of balanced reading based on more than 20 years of experience as a classroom teacher and more than 30 years of researching balanced approaches to reading instruction. As a result of these experiences and in the spirit of coming to a truly balanced, unbiased, ideological approach to teaching children how to read, the following definition is offered:

> A *balanced reading approach* is research-based, assessment-based, comprehensive, integrated, and dynamic, in that it empowers teachers and specialists to respond to the individual assessed literacy needs of children as they relate to their appropriate instructional and developmental levels of decoding, vocabulary, reading comprehension, motivation, and sociocultural acquisition, with the purpose of learning to read for meaning, understanding, and joy.

Teachers continue to grow and to learn by engaging in the tension of theory and practice as it is revealed to us more clearly through research; consequently, we are inspired and committed to teach, using everything that is necessary to help children learn to read successfully. In the final analysis, it is my belief that a balanced approach to beginning reading instruction, supported by the six major U.S. research studies, can help us to put the "reading wars" to rest.

CHAPTER 2

The Cooperative Research Program in First-Grade Reading Instruction (the First-Grade Studies)

(Guy L. Bond & Robert Dykstra, 1967/1997)

G uy L. Bond and Robert Dykstra's *Cooperative Research Program in First-Grade Reading Instruction* (the First-Grade Studies) (1967/1997) is one of the earliest comprehensive studies in the history of how young children begin to learn how to read. In fact, 27 individual projects were undertaken and coordinated by 27 different directors, in which a cadre of researchers compared first-grade reading programs from 1964 to 1967. The Cold War and ensuing fear and public opinion formed the underlying impetus and perceived need for the First-Grade Studies. In addition, the aftermath of Rudolph Flesch's (1955) *Why Johnny Can't Read*, the launching of Sputnik by the Russians in 1957, and the perception that the U.S. education system was losing ground to Russia's—a possible threat to U.S. defense security—prompted the U.S. Congress to pass the National Defense Education Act, which would channel funds to bolster the nation's education programs, including reading improvement.

As early as 1959, at a meeting of the National Conference on Research in English (at which Jeanne Chall and Guy Bond were present), a special committee on reading research was established, which was the precursor to the studies that Bond and Dykstra would head. At the meeting it was agreed that the available research on reading at that time was "so vague, contradictory, and incomplete as to encourage conflicting interpretations" (Graves & Dykstra, 1997, p. 343). It was agreed also that two complementary studies should be undertaken: Chall would conduct a critical, systematic analysis of the research already available (see chapter 3), and the group as a whole would undertake a more experimental approach to compare the existing methods of reading instruction, which would determine whether some instructional approaches were more effective than others in teaching first graders how to read (Graves & Dykstra, 1997). It is important to note that at the time Bond and Dykstra's research was being conducted (during the late 1950s and mid-1960s), the United States was in the midst of social and civil upheaval. In a highly critical and poignant commentary, Willis and Harris (1997) declared that the First-Grade Studies apparently ignored the underlying message and spirit of the times. They pointed out that while the U.S. Congress and President Lyndon Johnson were passing legislation to end school segregation and promising a "War on Poverty," the First-Grade Studies conducted very few investigations on marginal populations. Except for Chall's study of reading in socially disadvantaged neighborhoods in New York City when she served as a project director for the First-Grade Studies, other investigations were either discontinued or not reported because the researchers agreed that they did not fit the established criteria; for instance, "The establishment of these...criteria eliminated atypical populations such as those comprised of Spanish-speaking youngsters..." (Bond & Dykstra, 1997, p. 368). Further, although protests against U.S. involvement in Vietnam also were being waged at this time, it seemed to have no direct bearing on the First-Grade Studies either.

Bond and Dykstra, who coordinated the massive undertaking of the studies, employed a comparison-research design to examine the effectiveness of existing alternative reading programs and, concurrently, to investigate how students, teachers, schools, and communities may also contribute to the reading achievement of first-grade children.

Three Research Questions

In formulating the design of the First-Grade Studies, three research questions were posed to gather data and obtain information on beginning reading from which the study's findings and conclusions are drawn:

1. To what extent are various pupil, teacher, class, school, and community characteristics related to pupil achievement in first-grade reading and spelling?
2. Which of the many approaches to initial reading instruction produces superior reading and spelling achievement at the end of the first grade?
3. Is any program uniquely effective or ineffective for pupils with high or low readiness for reading? (1997, p. 348)

Research Question 1: To what extent are various pupil, teacher, class, school, and community characteristics related to pupil achievement in first-grade reading and spelling?

The researchers studied several teacher characteristics that were quantifiable, including age, gender, degrees earned, certification, teaching experience, years teaching first grade, attitudes toward teaching, and recorded absences during the study; even teacher marital status was considered. Student characteristics studied included age, gender, absentee rate, and class size. Even nonquantifiable data and information were analyzed about school and community characteristics. In short, the answer to this first research question is that student, teacher, class, school, and community characteristics related to reading and spelling achievement were negligible. Bond and Dykstra concluded that none of the teacher, student, or class characteristics are "highly related" (1997, p. 367) to reading or spelling achievement, and that there is little indication that school and community relationships are significant factors either. In response to this finding, Bond and Dykstra concluded that "To improve reading instruction, it is necessary to train better teachers of reading rather than to expect a panacea in the form of [methods and] materials" (p. 416). This insight provided a necessary impetus for future staff development research—which we will see later, began shortly thereafter and has continued its momentum in recent years. In hindsight, the results of this study also put an end to comparative studies of reading methodologies for some time to come.

Prior to the First-Grade Studies, research did not focus on how teachers interacted with children in the classroom. It was thought that all teachers of beginning reading taught in a fairly standardized way.

This investigation, however, proved different. At least one of the research projects examined teacher training relevant to student reading and spelling improvement. Arthur W. Hillman—a First-Grade Studies researcher and director—investigated the effects of an intensive inservice program on teachers' classroom behavior and students' reading achievement, finding that teachers can make a difference if properly trained in reading strategies. It is interesting to note that more than 30 years later, the National Reading Panel report (NICHD, 2000) makes a recommendation that is quite similar to the one made by the First-Grade Studies, indicating that staff development in literacy for teachers is related to improvement of student achievement in reading, spelling, and comprehension. Shortly after publication of the First-Grade Studies, researchers began investigating teacher and student behaviors in the classroom, which have continued to this day (Bruce & Showers, as cited in Cowen, 2001; NICHD, 2000; Snow, Burns, & Griffin, 1998).

To answer the question Does staff development in early childhood literacy instruction make a difference? I conducted an action research study that provided staff development in literacy for the purpose of changing teacher behaviors in order to improve beginning readers' literacy achievement (Cowen, 2001). This action research model began by building a knowledge and research base for teacher participants and empowering them to return to the classroom as teacher action researchers to apply theoretical models and demonstrated best practices in their classrooms. The results of this study showed that teacher behavior and instructional practices can change once participants are empowered to engage in a dynamic action-research process that leads to self-improvement. Consequently, this change in behavior enables the teacher to learn how to teach reading more effectively, resulting in improved literacy achievement for young children (Cowen, 2001).

Bruce Joyce and Beverly Showers's (as cited in Cowen, 2001) research on staff development indicates that a successful inservice model should include at least four important components: theory, demonstration, practice, and coaching. These research findings also show that in each of the four components, "the skills acquired by staff development participants are lowest when only theory is presented

(10–20%); whereas, skills acquired increases to 35% with demonstration, and increases significantly to 75% when combined with theory, demonstration, and practice" (p. 52). When the coaching component is combined with theory, demonstration, and practice, the skills acquired by these staff development participants increases to a very high level of significance, reported by Bruce and Showers to be 90%.

Although the First-Grade Studies did not find that class size influenced reading or spelling achievement significantly, Bond and Dykstra (1967/1997) explain that the experimental classrooms used in the study were neither too large nor too small. More recent, larger longitudinal studies (Tennessee's STAR and Wisconsin's SAGE program as cited in Biddle & Berliner, 2002), however, have demonstrated that class size can actually make a difference. Smaller class size in the primary grades does relate to children's achievement in early literacy, particularly for disadvantaged children, but only when the number of students in the classroom does not exceed 15, according to the SAGE study's findings; whereas, the STAR study's class enrollments averaged 20 students for each teacher. Prior to 1967, however, class size had not been an issue that received much attention by researchers; therefore, studies with regard to class size since 1967 can be traced back to the First-Grade Studies. With the advent of state and national standards for the English language arts and high-stakes testing, there recently has been a great deal of revived interest in class size and school size.

Finally, though Bond and Dykstra indicate that there was no conclusive evidence that school or community were significant factors in student literacy achievement, their explanation for this is somewhat vague, and the rationale given is related to difficulties in controlling statistical results drawn from the various projects. For instance, Bond and Dykstra explain that

> there was little indication that any of the school and community characteristics were significantly related to the reading achievement. This statement of no relationship, of course is valid only with reference to the specific communities, schools, and school populations included in this project. Furthermore, many of the community characteristics were categorized in such a way as to make it difficult to use them as control variables in a covariance analysis. (1997, p. 360)

Based on this statement, it appears that the majority of communities and schools targeted in this project were more or less homogeneous. Therefore, it causes conjecture as to whether this lack of significance related to reading is the result of the data being collected from various sites that could not be contrasted with populations more diverse in terms of poverty, race, culture, and linguistic backgrounds. In contrast to these findings, for instance, *Preventing Reading Difficulties in Young Children* (1998) and the National Reading Panel report (NICHD, 2000) show that the major differences are that children in communities and schools, particularly in low-socioeconomic urban areas, "are at risk of arriving at school with weaknesses in these areas and hence of falling behind from the outset" (1998, p. 5). Nevertheless, the First-Grade Studies investigation of this important relationship of school and community and reading achievement is noteworthy and continues to be an important issue for researchers.

Research Question 2: Which of the many approaches to initial reading instruction produces superior reading and spelling achievement at the end of the first grade?

The First-Grade Studies (1967/1997) compares several innovative literacy approaches to the basal reader and to several combination approaches (basal readers plus one or more innovative literacy approaches).

> Six types of instructional materials or methods were used as experimental treatments in more than one project.... Five separate analyses were then performed, each analysis using the basal reader as a control against which to compare progress in other instructional programs. All of the projects which used as experimental treatments both a basal reader approach and an i.t.a. [Initial Teaching Alphabet] approach, for example, were combined into a single analysis. (1997, p. 368)

1. Initial Teaching Alphabet
2. Basal Plus Phonics
3. Language Experience
4. Linguistic
5. Phonic/Linguistic
6. Basal (alone)

The six groupings were used as experimental treatments by the researchers and included more than one project. The above-mentioned alternative reading approaches of the day were compared to teachers using the basal reader, teachers using a basal plus phonics approach, or a combination approach to beginning reading instruction. The popular basal reading programs of the 1960s featured a controlled vocabulary; a teacher-proof, scripted teacher's manual; and a classroom instructional management system relegated to teaching children in three distinct reading-leveled groups (Snow, Burns, & Griffin, 1998). However, phonics was taught sparingly in favor of instruction in high-frequency sight words, structural analysis features, meaning emphasis, and discourse about stories composed by academics rather than authors of authentic children's literature. As mentioned, the controlled vocabulary, a feature of most basal reading series, limited the number of words to which children could be introduced. This small sampling of words was determined by the frequency with which these words appeared in a limited number of children's books, despite the fact that a majority of children had accumulated an oral vocabulary that included hundreds of words in contrast to the limited number of words featured in the basal reading series studied (Chall, 1967).

In response to Question 2, it was concluded that classrooms using an integrated approach, which combined systematic phonics with reading for meaning and writing, far surpassed those using mainstream basal programs. The favoring of a more comprehensive program, which included phonics, reading meaningful text, and reading and writing for meaning, illustrates how the research findings in this study support a more balanced approach to reading instruction in contrast to the basal-alone approach. The study, however, did not champion any one specific method of phonics instruction, as is the case with the subsequent studies. In fact, Bond and Dykstra concluded that

> children learn to read by a variety of materials and methods. Pupils become successful readers in such vastly different programs as the Language Experience approach with its relative lack of structure and vocabulary control and the various Linguistic programs with their relatively high degree of structure and vocabulary control. Furthermore, pupils experienced difficulty in each of the programs utilized. (1997, p. 416)

Bond and Dykstra are far more authoritative in their final concluding statement and summative response to Question 2, stating, "No one approach is so distinctly better in all situations and respects than the others that it should be considered the one best method and the one to be used exclusively" (p. 416).

Notably, the First-Grade Studies is one of the first U.S. national research reports to point to the advantage of using an early code-emphasis (Snow, Burns, & Griffin, 1998), which is quite similar to Chall's (1967) findings, showing that systematic, early code instruction improves children's spelling and comprehension. Bond and Dykstra's (1997) analyses also indicated that approaches that included systematic phonics instruction far exceeded the use of straight basal programs in word recognition achievement. Furthermore, in support of a balanced reading approach, these researchers concluded that when combined approaches included systematic phonics and an emphasis on connected reading and meaning, these integrated approaches significantly surpassed the basal-alone approaches. A very similar refrain will be heard throughout the five remaining studies to be discussed in this book.

Research Question 3: Is any program uniquely effective or ineffective for pupils with high or low readiness for reading?

The readiness tests administered to children entering first grade were the standardized evaluation measures teachers often used to establish reading groups and to determine student retention in kindergarten, because these children were deemed to lack the readiness or prerequisite skills to begin first grade. To the surprise of the First-Grade Studies' project researchers, conflicting information and results from the data and analyses were occurring from site-to-site despite their careful efforts to account for such problems. Bond and Dykstra, responding to this point, state that

> one of the most striking findings was the persistence of project differ-
> ences in reading achievement, even after adjustments were made sta-
> tistically for differences in pupil readiness for reading. Evidently,
> reading achievement is influenced by factors peculiar to school sys-
> tems over and above differences in prereading capabilities of pupils.
> (1997, p. 415)

Even though the researchers could not answer with any degree of certainty why no specific program was uniquely effective or ineffective with regard to student readiness, a scientific discovery of perhaps even greater value was revealed as an epiphany. That is, from that moment on, there would need to be a paradigm shift away from "reading readiness" to a whole new concept of literacy that would evolve to what we now refer to as "emergent literacy." No longer would kindergarten teachers teach a program designed specifically for reading readiness with a belief that children came to school as blank slates. Instead, we discovered that children begin learning about literacy during infancy and continue their emergence as readers and writers long before they enter school.

Another startling finding and breakthrough in beginning reading reported by Bond and Dykstra is that "Obviously, the ability to recognize letters at the beginning of first grade was related to reading success in all of the methods and programs employed in the study" (1997, p. 365). The importance of children learning the letters of the alphabet produced the single most predictive relationship to future success in reading. The second most important predictive relationship to future success in reading was the "Phonic/Linguistic treatment where the Phonemes test correlated best" (p. 365). Although Marilyn Jager Adams is often credited for the advancement of phonemic awareness and its importance in beginning reading, it is important to note that the First-Grade Studies produced two important and lasting scientifically proven findings. Simply put, convergent research over 30 years verifies that the two most important predictors for beginning students' success in learning to read are (1) "Knowledge of Letter Names" [Alphabetic Principle] and (2) "Ability to discriminate between word sounds" [Phonemic Awareness] (1997, p. 413). Bond and Dykstra also recommend that an informal assessment using only letter names from the alphabet is an excellent and valid predictor of reading success. Clay's (1993) "Observation Survey" continues to provide a simple format for assessing children's letter identification ability (a valid predictor of successful reading) to inform teachers of students' instructional needs in this vital area.

Strengths of the Study

The First-Grade Studies influenced the research of beginning reading for the next 30 years. It may be that the ancillary discoveries made while answering the three research questions that guided this research study form the legacy for which it will be best remembered. For instance, future studies began investigating the role of the teacher and classrooms rather than centering on comparisons of methods and materials. Future interest related to professional development in literacy for classroom teachers is a consequence of this research study, and staff development continues to be of major importance today. The concept of reading readiness questioned as a result of this study also helped refocus future theorists and researchers' inquiries, enabling them to go beyond this traditional, yet inadequate, concept (Clay, 1993). Consequently, a broader, more encompassing and meaningful concept—emergent literacy—was developed and continues to influence our profession's thinking today. As mentioned earlier, the verification that beginning readers must first learn the letter names of the alphabet and, next, learn how to distinguish phonemes or letter sounds has given rise to the importance of phonemic awareness. The study of certain innovative methods—particularly linguistics, Language Experience Approach (LEA), and Initial Teaching Alphabet (ITA)—depicted how children's knowledge of phonemes and identifying corresponding sounds in words developed more rapidly as a result of frequent writing and discovery through word construction. Such conclusions predate later findings about the importance of invented spelling and invented writing activities that have helped advance children's learning of phonics. Also, conclusions that systematic phonics is a necessary and effective way to teach all children to read, regardless of method, are a major contribution to the field of reading and have continued to produce numerous related studies. It is also important to note that Bond and Dykstra showed that systematic phonics worked regardless of students' socioeconomic status. Teaching children more words, at a faster pace, also questioned the value of controlled vocabulary formats. The researchers' conclusion that basal-alone methods did not fare well in comparison to other approaches, which combined phonics or other innovative code-based methods, proves that a sight-word approach to reading is less effective. Finally, it is important to note that Bond and Dykstra's findings and conclusions with regard to the importance of knowing letter names, phonemes, and phonics paralleled and verified Chall's (1967) discoveries, nonetheless, using a different research method.

Limitations of the Study

Although this study is often referenced for its historical importance, it is unfortunate according to Snow, Burns, and Griffin (1998) that, perhaps due to several mitigating circumstances, including unavailable studies from cross-disciplinary research still to be published, "these studies were not submitted to the levels of analysis characteristic of later efforts" (p. 173). The findings and conclusions from the study seem not as apparent as they might be, perhaps because the reporting format is not reader friendly because it does not provide a simple, organized delineation of the analyses or direct reference to each of the three research questions that the report sets out to answer. Also, except for brief summaries and a list of conclusions, Bond and Dykstra do not provide a discussion section to help readers project how the findings of this study could be useful to practitioners or to recommend how some ancillary findings might require further investigation. Pearson (1999) seems to echo this sentiment somewhat in stating, "[In 1967] we were trying to ferret out the implications of the First-Grade Studies" (p. 231). As mentioned earlier, the massive number of programs, students, and teachers studied had to be an enormous coordination problem. To maintain fidelity of so many varied treatments, to cull out and analyze an unwieldy data collection (without the benefit of personal computers), and to control the evenness of reporting from site to site—even though much coordination effort and planning took place prior to, during, and after these investigations began—had to be a researcher's nightmare. It is not inconsequential, therefore, that the First-Grade Studies has not received, until recently, the accolades that Chall's (1967) *Learning to Read: The Great Debate* did when it was published at about the same time (Adams, 1990a). However, this is not to say that Chall's research methodology was not criticized as well. This will be discussed in greater detail in chapter 3 (Rutherford, as cited in Adams, 1990a; Strickland, 1998).

CHAPTER 3

Learning to Read: The Great Debate
(Jeanne S. Chall, 1967)

Jeanne S. Chall's classic study on early reading practices was conducted from 1962 to 1965. Like Bond and Dykstra (1967), Chall admits that she was influenced to a large degree by fears in the United States that the Russians were ahead in education and winning the space race following their successful launching of the Sputnik satellite. Also, the literacy community was still reeling from *Why Johnny Can't Read* (Flesch, 1955), which was an indictment of U.S. public schools, claiming that U.S. children were not learning how to read as well as Russian children because they were not being taught phonics. Chall (1967) explains that although Flesch's book received favorable notices in the media, his information was erroneous, and his sensational claims were not supported by research in professional reading journals. Nevertheless, the questions Flesch's book raised fanned the fires of newly waged reading wars of the times and, therefore, received a great deal of attention from politicians and the public. More than 30 years later, in fact, Chall would compare the days of *The Great Debate* to the present:

> As *RRQ* rightly noted, this was a time of great controversy in the teaching of beginning reading, quite similar to the controversy of the past decade. Indeed, it was the heated disagreements regarding the best way to teach beginners to read that convinced the Carnegie Corporation to sponsor my historical analysis and synthesis of past research and the U.S. Office of Education to sponsor the First-Grade Studies. (1999, p. 8)

Not only was the literacy field at this time scrambling to find out causes for an apparent downward slide in national reading scores, but, on another front, the discipline's curriculum reform movement (Phoenix, 1964) had evolved, calling for more rigorous programs in science and mathematics. Schaefer (1967) was one of the early advocates for developing the school as a center of inquiry for children, while a frenzy of curricula reforms were being ushered in throughout the 1960s and 1970s, which were perceived as national priorities. Benjamin S. Bloom, chair of the American Psychology Association, had begun conducting studies advocating the improvement of student comprehension, which was thought to be unchallenged as a result of low academic expectations and a diet of rote learning. Bloom's (1956) influential study *Taxonomy of Educational Objectives: Part I, Cognitive Domain* was the result of this work. In this book, he introduced a hierarchy of six levels of thinking skills, beginning at the lowest level, rote learning, to the highest thinking level, evaluation. Higher order thinking skills soon became the psychological defense for a jittery nation during the 1960s at the height of the Cold War.

Meanwhile, Chall, a professor at City University of New York (and later at Harvard University's Graduate School of Education), was busy conducting a comprehensive and scholarly analysis of the available research on practices in classroom reading instruction. To help inform her data analysis, Chall began conducting investigations in the field, including (1) classroom observations across the United States, as well as in England and Scotland; (2) personal interviews with reading experts, teachers, administrators, and publishers; and (3) documentation and analyses of a variety of existing reading programs, including the prevailing basal reading programs of the day (Chall, 1967).

In terms of the debate, Chall set out to answer the question Do children learn better with a beginning method that stresses meaning or with one that stresses learning the code? Her findings showed overwhelming support for those beginning programs that "included systematic phonics" (1967, p. 75). In grades 1 through 3, systematic code outcomes were stunningly better in word recognition, spelling, vocabulary, and reading comprehension. The study further clarified that a phonics approach was superior to the whole-word approach or the look-say method prevalently in use by most basal readers (Chall, 1967; Snow, Burns, & Griffin, 1998). At the same time, Chall did not recommend any one particular phonics approach, and although she supported an early code emphasis, she did not intend that to "displace an emphasis on reading for meaning" (p. 239). Moreover, according to *Preventing Reading Difficulties in Young Children* (PRD) (Snow,

Burns, & Griffin, 1998), "the advantage of systematic phonics was just as great and perhaps greater for children from lower socioeconomic backgrounds or with low-level abilities entering first grade as it was for better prepared or more privileged children" (pp. 173–174). Chall's findings are particularly relevant today considering the ever-growing disparity reported by PRD and by the National Reading Panel (NICHD, 2000), which have compared Caucasian students' reading achievement to African American and Latino students' reading achievement, especially those from large urban, inner-city backgrounds.

It is also quite striking that the findings and recommendations of Chall's study are so similar to that of Bond and Dykstra's (1967/1997), even though each was conducted independently using very different research methodologies. While Chall reviewed more than 50 years of relevant existing research, and Bond and Dykstra compared various reading methods using a more experimental, scientific research design, the results of the two studies, as well as their recommendations, were quite congruent (Chall, 1999). In fact, Chall's findings, like Bond and Dykstra's, offered the following conclusions:

- Stronger, more systematic phonics or decoding programs produced higher reading achievement.
- Basal series that focused largely on reading for meaning were inferior to stronger phonics programs or approaches.
- Learning the alphabetic code was essential in beginning reading.
- Phonics, word analysis, decoding, and sound-symbol relations (alphabetic code) were essential, but not all were necessary to be successful in learning how to read.
- Language, good teaching and instructional materials on an appropriate level of difficulty are important factors in producing high reading achievement.
- A stronger phonics emphasis to beginning reading proved more effective, especially for low-socioeconomic status children.

Chall (1967) is also one of the first researchers to point out the importance of extensive reading for developing fluency and understanding, as well as the need to practice reading challenging texts to develop a fuller understanding of these newly acquired skills. Chall also advocated the early use of direct, explicit instruction of the code prior to practicing those skills (with a meaning emphasis soon to follow) through literature, writing, and comprehension. To be sure, Chall did not advocate teaching skills for skills' sake, but insisted that a measured balance is required. To illustrate this point, Chall emphasizes that

> the existing evidence seems to indicate that each stage of reading requires a different *balance of skills* [emphasis added] versus application with the earlier levels needing relatively more direct teaching of skills. But even here, applications are needed through listening to stories, through oral reading of stories and plays and the like. Thus, although the skills are necessary for most children, and a stronger emphasis on skills is needed in the earlier grades the humanistic aspects must not be forgotten even then. (1980, p. 58)

Chall's view of balance is also evident in her statement, "No program can do all things for all children, and no program can be all things for all teachers" (1967, p. 310), but she advocated that teachers receive adequate staff development before they were asked by superiors to change over to a code-emphasis beginning reading program. In some schools that Chall visited, she was informed that teachers actually threatened to resign rather than have to teach with a code emphasis. She lamented that these teachers were forced to teach with a code emphasis without being informed and without benefit of a "research and development framework" (p. 310). Chall was also sympathetic to teachers who had been successful in teaching children to read and who were knowledgeable about reading and diagnosis. She believed that such teachers should continue teaching without having to change and that such needless adjustments might actually destroy the beauty of what the teacher was achieving in teaching her students to read. Chall, however, seemed more intent on changing or modifying the prevailing basal reading series guidebooks and teacher manuals that stressed the teaching of whole words and configurations and that limited the teaching of phonics or code emphasis. Chall, for instance, states that she believes that authors and publishers of basal series can play a major role in adjusting instruction to be in line with the available research evidence that she and the First-Grade Studies' findings reported.

Chall also spoke candidly about the content in stories that should be related to children's background knowledge and familiarity. She indicated that the content and story line of the basal readers ignored nonwhite urban children. And, although she believed that a change in content should be considered, Chall was convinced that the evidence of her research showed that a code-emphasis start for nonwhite children was probably more important than a change in content, which, until then, had not been substantiated. Her personal content preference for teaching children of diverse backgrounds (and for all first and second graders) was to use folktales and fairy tales that had universal appeal. As Chall states, "I never found one who could not identify with 'Cinderella,' 'The Gingerbread Boy,' or 'The Three Little Pigs.' These tales contain struggle and triumph, right and wrong, laughter and tears—themes that have disappeared from modern stories based on familiar experiences" (1967, p. 312). Chall's investigations in the classrooms also helped her conclude that teachers did not have to fear that initial code emphasis would destroy children's enjoyment of reading or that children would become "word callers" who could not read for meaning. Instead, her research findings showed that children who learned from the code at the beginning read with better comprehension and reading enjoyment. Chall also was quick to point out that the code should be emphasized only as a beginning reading method and that reading for meaning had to be stressed thereafter. In her advocacy of a balanced approach to reading instruction, Chall writes emphatically, "Once the pupil has learned to recognize in print the words he knows (because they are part of his speaking and listening vocabulary), any additional work on decoding is a sheer waste of time" (p. 307). Finally, Chall emphasizes that there is no evidence for endorsing any one code-emphasis method over another and that, like the First-Grade Studies had concluded, a number of code programs, for instance, linguistics, initial teaching alphabet, and systematic-phonics, were no better or worse than any other. She recommended moving away from a meaning-emphasis method to a code-emphasis method for beginning instruction only.

Strengths of the Study

One may look back at *Learning to Read: The Great Debate* and at the First-Grade Studies and reach the conclusion that these two seminal studies set a course for decades of future research in beginning reading. Much of what has been reported of a balanced reading program in the findings of these studies remains irrefutable to this day. In spite of some criticism regarding Chall's arbitrary division of programs into code- and meaning emphasis, her report on effective reading practices is still considered to be one of the great classics in contemporary research (Adams, 1990a; Burns, Snow, & Griffin, 1998). Chall's conclusions not only validated the First-Grade Studies research, but they proved emphatically that systematic phonics had major advantages over meaning-driven, basal-reader-dominated instruction. Also, these conclusions were measured by outcomes from several major areas including decoding, vocabulary, spelling, and comprehension through third grade. Chall's personal investigation of schools in the United Kingdom also reported how children can begin learning the code as early as kindergarten, whereas in the United States, educators were still worried that introduction to the code in first grade was too early and potentially destructive. There has been a great deal of interest recently in teaching phonemic awareness and other related beginning reading skills in kindergarten. Much of the results has been positive and has led to children's early interest and love of reading (Adams, 1990a; Anderson et al., 1985; NICHD, 2000; Snow, Burns, & Griffin, 1998).

Chall's investigations related to lower socioeconomic children and to children with lower level abilities showed that early code emphasis proved most beneficial to this growing at-risk population. This major finding is important to this day, particularly with regard to the published reports of existing disparity in terms of reading achievement among nonwhite and white children, and especially of those children living in poor urban settings across the United States. Chall's research also set the course for future studies with regard to the importance of reading fluency as it relates to the development of reading comprehension. Her view that advocating that children read challenging literature raises vocabulary achievement and, subsequently, reading comprehension is also a major finding, as well as her conclusion that children need to practice newly introduced reading skills by using texts that can be read independently. Chall also concluded that early code emphasis not only improves word recognition, but that it also improves children's spelling ability and reading comprehension achievement. Bond and Dykstra apparently did not draw this same conclusion relative to this vital area until one year after reading Chall's study. More recently, Bear and his colleagues (2000) reported that research studies related to student development in spelling were highly correlated with students' improvement in their overall reading development. Similarly, the National Reading Panel (2000) reported that reading comprehension improvement was greatly attributable to vocabulary and fluency improvement, further verification of Chall's findings.

Limitations of the Study

Chall received mostly accolades for her study; however, her methodology was criticized for her examination of often dated studies notwithstanding her limitations due to a lack of available modern statistical techniques. Chall's research methodology also has been criticized for having some design flaws inherent in the study itself and what Strickland (1998) refers to as her "arbitrary coding" system (Rutherford, as cited in Adams, 1990a, p. 9). Perhaps, few if any research studies can be reported without some modicum of deficiencies, and Chall's study was no exception. Rutherford (as cited in Adams, 1990a), for instance, criticized Chall for her coding system that divided code-emphasized and meaning-emphasized approaches in her attempt to show how early code emphasis had a more positive effect on beginning reading achievement compared to basal readers, which placed greater emphasis on meaning and learning sight words before children were taught how to sound out unfamiliar words. Perhaps Chall's insistence on a code-first approach (which seemed arbitrary to more holistic, literature-minded teachers of the time) as opposed to studying a more seamless code-sight-word-meaning combination approach, might have heightened an already charged environment of debate, resulting in greater alienation by those more inclined toward balance. Naturally, Chall's intention was to heighten everyone's awareness, particularly that of the basal writers and publishers in order to impress on them the need for making major adjustments in an emphasis away from meaning toward a more systematic code or phonics approach. To some degree this was accomplished, although today it is evident that the basal publishers have not made the sweeping changes Chall had expected as a result of her report. Yet, basal reading series continue to be the dominating reading materials sold to U.S. schools. At times, some of Chall's statements on phonics instruction must have irritated the opposing camp, with such rhetorical statements as, "The little children I watched were as excited and keenly interested in words, sounds, spellings and rules as they were in stories" (p. 270). Similarly, some teachers might especially take exception to the following statement in which Chall is apparently trying to convince teachers that children are not opposed to being taught skills such as phonics: "My conclusion was that children can become interested in anything" (p. 271). On the other hand, Chall does indicate that (although the evidence was not entirely clear) certain systematic phonics approaches could lead to "dull drill" (p. 271). Chall reports having observed some teachers using words that were too difficult or inappropriate for this purpose, resulting in children losing interest.

Finally, although it is important for researchers to conduct on-site visits to observe students learning and teachers instructing as Chall had done, it is also difficult for the participant observer to objectify or filter out that which is being observed impartially. This is, perhaps, most difficult when the observer is interpreting a particular phenomenon, especially when faced with deciding objectively for or against its efficacy, particularly if the prevailing viewpoint in question is really your own.

In retrospect, Chall's study is a classical one, so carefully conducted, so well conceived, and so well written that it has few limitations worth noting. In fact, it stands today as one of the most prominent reading studies, comparing favorably to and in the same light as Adams's (1990a) study *Beginning to Read.*

CHAPTER 4

Becoming a Nation of Readers: The Report of the Commission on Reading

(Richard C. Anderson, Elfrieda H. Hiebert, Judith A. Scott, & Ian A.G. Wilkinson, 1985)

Two years after the National Commission on Excellence in Education (NCEE) (1983) released its highly critical report of U.S. schools, *A Nation at Risk: The Imperative for Educational Reform*, *Becoming a Nation of Readers* (BNR) (1985) appeared, apparently in direct response to the former volume's general criticism of widespread literacy problems in the United States.

Political concerns of the 1980s—economic rather than military— became the catalyst for a new wave of educational criticism. A prime example of this criticism was *A Nation at Risk* (1983), which had addressed the lack of will and commitment on the part of the United States to remain the most preeminent nation economically, educationally, scientifically, and technologically. The inflammatory nature of the report jolted the nation into a frenzy of education reforms, including the formation of yet another reading synthesis study to determine once again why the youngest children in the United States were not all reading on grade level.

Economic concerns such as rising inflation, soaring interest rates, and Japanese economic domination were apparently the impetus for the National Academy of Education, National Institute of Education, and Center for the Study of Reading to sponsor the most significant literacy research study since the 1960s. The early 1980s was also a period in which education's most severe critics were calling for "a return to the basics." Illustrative of these times is a *New York Times Magazine* article, "How Schools Fail Our Children," by Frank F. Ambusher (August 29, 1977, cited in Cowen 1980):

> It is true that, in many ways this means returning to a system we had 20 years and three-quarters of a trillion tax dollars ago. This is certainly a bitter pill for us to swallow, but with the welfare of a generation of youngsters at stake, we may have no other choice. (p. 52)

Richard Anderson, Elfrieda Hiebert, Judith Scott, and Ian Wilkinson (1985), authors of BNR, worked in tandem with the National Academy of Education's Commission on Reading, a scholarly advisory group that included several literacy experts in the field such as Jeanne Chall (see chapter 3). Chall's presence was expressed in a direct way when she wrote in the book's afterword that BNR had not addressed children's specific learning disabilities adequately, and the report basically ignored the adult illiteracy problem that was gripping the United States.

With regard to research design, the studies of the 1980s provided much more technological advances compared to those conducted in the 1960s; consequently, Anderson and colleagues made three broad areas of inquiry into the cognition of language psychology: (1) linguistics, (2) child development, and (3) behavioral science. Like its predecessors, BNR points to the importance of teaching the alphabetic system early as a basis for developing word recognition. These researchers were the first to report on the significant importance of automatic word recognition, later to be emphasized in Adams's (1990a) research in which she discusses the importance of "automaticity" and fluency related to reading for meaning. BNR's conclusions, related to the importance of text structure and its influence in teaching reading comprehension, is also important as a precursor to later studies and conclusions drawn by the National Reading Panel (NICHD, 2000). Anderson et al. (1985) stress the importance of a balanced reading approach by stating rather boldly that phonics should be taught early, that teachers should keep it simple, and phonics need not be taught beyond the end of second grade for most children. Although the researchers identify the value of teaching phonemic awareness, they do not stress its importance quite like Adams (1990a) does in her study. However, the study indicates that the goal of phonics is to teach children the alphabetic principle and that they should be able to see the relationship between the letters and sounds and, therefore, begin to sound out letters to blend words. BNR also states that it is no longer a question of whether children should be taught phonics, but rather it is a question of how this instruction should be done. These researchers also conclude that children who are taught phonics learn to read faster than those who are not taught phonics explicitly. BNR stresses the importance of reading for meaning more than the other studies but not at the expense of developing a balanced approach to reading instruction that includes learning the alphabetic principle and phonics through grade 2. Most important, BNR concludes that children should read words in meaningful texts and that comprehension will come when children have lots of opportunities to read enjoyable texts at their independent reading level. The researchers concluded that developing interest and motivation in reading is necessary and that writing and reading good literature will help children become lifetime readers.

Although the two studies conducted in 1967 (see chapters 2 and 3) did not favor any one reading method over another, Anderson and colleagues do recommend specified approaches. According to Pearson (1999), the combined phonics strategies recommended in BNR favor a balanced approach that promotes skillful, fluent, and meaningful reading. The study also points out that phonics can be taught best using a combined approach that includes (1) synthetic phonics (a direct, sequential approach); (2) analogy (an embedded, indirect analysis); and (3) phonics in context. The Commission's recommendations favoring a combined phonics approach are identified and labeled according to the following three useful phonics approaches:

- Teaching sounds of letters in isolation (1)
- Teaching sounds of letters in words (1)
- Teaching how to blend sounds of letters to approximate words (2)
- Identifying words of similar spellings (2)
- Identifying words in meaningful sentences and stories (3)

With regard to early reading texts, Anderson et al. specify that to be instructive "primers must contain words that can be identified using phonics that has already been taught. There is a natural relationship between word identification and comprehension" (pp. 58–59). The report also recommends that these texts be interesting and comprehensible and should tell complete and interesting stories. This is in contrast to earlier texts for beginning readers written in a controlled vocabulary and limited to only 12 or so words such as *The New Fun With Dick and Jane* series. These primer stories produced an unnatural, nearly incomprehensible dialogue as shown in the following example:

"Look, Mother," said Sally.

"Red, yellow, blue!"

"Look, Mother," said Jane.

"We look pretty."

"Oh, yes," said Mother.

"Yes, Jane, yes!

You look pretty.

Sally looks pretty, too."

From *The New Fun With Dick and Jane*, Primer, New Basic Readers Series. Copyright ©1956 by Scott, Foresman. (See Chall, 1967, p. 223.)

The BNR report also extols the value of and the need for wide reading of authentic literature; the reciprocal benefit of authentic writing to reading improvement is also stressed throughout the study. The researchers also support the need for developing early reading strategies such as self-monitoring and self-correcting reading by learning to read for meaning. BNR is also the first report to fully recognize the reciprocal value and importance of writing and reading. It may be that during the 1980s, writing had captured the interest of a number of researchers, most notably Donald Graves (1983), whose research began by examining writing as it was being taught in classrooms, and by comparing the teaching of writing to the way professional writers actually wrote. Other researchers and authors such as MacDonald, Fletcher, and McCormack-Calkins took up Graves's interest in writing research, which in the 1980s became popular instructional classroom approaches known as the writing-process approach and the writing-workshop approach.

One of BNR's most quoted reported findings is related to the inordinate amount of time children were spending filling out mindless and often unrelated workbook pages. In fact, BNR researchers reported that young readers were spending only 7 to 8 minutes per day reading independently, while older students through eighth grade spent as little as 15 minutes per day reading independently. Psycholinguist Frank Smith (1984), on the other hand, reports that in order for children to learn how to read, they must read several times daily, silently, and orally, and read for prolonged periods of quality time. Studies show that time spent filling out worksheets without teacher intervention has little impact on reading achievement and may even retard improvement (Tompkins, 1997). The BNR researchers supported an integrated language arts approach to reading development, stating that students should be engaged in reading and writing instead of the time spent on workbook pages. The researchers' recommendations were especially emphatic about the need for teaching more writing and the need for students to spend more time writing in the classroom, because "research showed that less than 15% of the school day was given over to writing in grades one, three, and five" (p. 79). The report also showed that little direct teaching of reading comprehension occurred in classrooms across the United States, although it was greatly needed. In fact, Anderson and colleagues developed five generalizations from their research findings, building on the concept that reading is an interactive process, not a passive one, while concluding that teachers must consider these principles while teaching beginning reading:

1. Reading is a constructive process and readers draw from prior knowledge while constructing meaning.

2. Reading must be fluent, beginning with identifying individual words rapidly with ease, or with automaticity (Adams, 1990a). Also, readers who read fluently also read sentences with a rhythm and intonation demonstrating that they are constructing meaning.

3. The readers' prior knowledge or familiarity with the topic and purpose for reading must be taken into account; also, reading must be strategic; therefore, readers must learn how to adjust and respond to the complexity of the text.

4. Reading requires motivation.

5. Reading is a continuously developing skill that continues to improve through practice.

A balanced approach to reading is strongly advocated throughout this report, and it is somewhat telling that Anderson and colleagues describe the reading process by comparing it to the performance of a symphonic orchestra in three movements (see Appendix A):

1. Reading takes place only when the parts are put together in a smooth, integrated performance.

2. Success in reading comes from practice over long periods of time, like skill in playing musical instruments.

3. As with a musical score, there may be more than one interpretation of a text.

In addition, Marilyn Jager Adams (1990a, 1990b) uses an automobile engine analogy to describe the reading process (see Appendix A). However, in both analogies, we see that for the reading process to function smoothly and effectively, it needs all the various complex parts to work together as one fine-tuned system.

BNR is very much in favor of seeking this balance and is the first major study or report to conclude that "the single most important activity for building the knowledge required for eventual success in reading is reading aloud to children" (p. 23). The researchers also write that "the ethos of the school should promote literacy" (p. 114). And, according to this group of researchers, the school should begin promoting literacy at a very early stage. For instance, the researchers conclude that children should learn to write what they say orally, as early as kindergarten. In fact, "the Commission favors a balanced Kindergarten Program in reading and language arts that includes both formal and informal approaches" (p. 29). In its final analysis, BNR calls for a program that is balanced and one that integrates skills throughout the reading process, starting from kindergarten throughout the elementary grades. The BNR researchers further conclude that "learning to read appears to involve close knitting of reading skills that complement and support one another, rather than learning one skill, adding a second, then a third, and so on" (p. 97). This conclusion shows how integration is central to a balanced reading approach that is also comprehensive and thoughtful.

Strengths of the Study

This balanced, integrated approach to beginning reading presented in this easy to read, sensitive report seems to have helped diffuse the anger, confusion, and fear created by *A Nation at Risk*. BNR is written with a confidence and poise that seems to say, "Don't worry, we've looked at the situation, and it's all under control; don't panic, things are not quite as bad as others might like us to think they are." The report simply verifies Bond and Dykstra's and Chall's research. BNR is more balanced, more whole language-like, perhaps because whole language and writing as a process was coming into its own. Nevertheless, the reading debates were rekindling once more, and the age-old concern that phonics would be out-played by meaning-first enthusiasts must have given the BNR researchers some cause for concern. Nevertheless, one of the major strengths of BNR is that no one approach is stressed over another, and indeed this is one of the first major reports to champion a common ground for phonics and a constructivist approach, which allows phonics and reading for meaning to coexist. Anderson and colleagues end the report by emphasizing that all reading studies depend on our best reading and classroom teachers, who are the key to providing outstanding reading instruction to children. These researchers call for future research studies that are also "balanced" in that they are capable of demonstrating through best practices and exemplary teaching how reading is taught. The exemplary first-grade studies conducted by Morrow, Tracey, Woo, and Pressley (1999) are the kind of balanced research studies envisioned by BNR researchers in light of their prophetic statement, "America will become a nation of readers when verified practices of the best teachers in the best schools can be introduced throughout the country" (1985, p. 120). To accomplish this goal, however, research methodologies will have to be more balanced, exploring qualitative action research designs along with experimental, scientific research.

Limitations of the Study

BNR appears to have neglected a major problem that the United States should have been addressing during this time: how to begin dealing with the reading disparity that the National Assessment of Educational Progress (NAEP) and other national and statewide tests had begun reporting during the 1980s. The 1984 NAEP test reported that growing numbers of minority children were having difficulty learning to read. Disparity issues related to reading achievement comparisons between white and nonwhite children began making headlines during the late 1970s and 1980s. The numbers of children entering the public schools speaking languages other than English were already posing major concerns for school administrators and classroom teachers. Nevertheless, BNR hardly addresses these pressing concerns nor does it address children who are at risk. It is quite interesting that Chall, who had also neglected these issues to some degree, now criticizes or at least takes a minority position in her afterword in BNR (1985). Chall begins by stating that she was concerned mostly about "persons who have serious reading difficulties" (p. 123). Chall goes on to say that millions of children and adults have special problems in learning to read, "especially from low income families, ethnic minorities, non–English or recent speakers of English and those with specific reading and learning disabilities" (p. 123). Although it is not entirely clear as to what Chall's purpose in writing this afterword was, it appears from one of her concluding comments that she had hoped

> that in order to effect a significant improvement in reading for children and adults with reading/learning disability, we will need to plan for more care, more funds, and more professional help both to prevent and treat their difficulties...if we are to truly become a nation of readers. (pp. 124–125)

BNR is a bridge between the pioneering research of Bond and Dykstra and Chall in the 1960s and Adams's integrated treatment of research of the 1990s. BNR encourages us as reading professionals to help children think about reading that goes beyond proficiency in order to extend their literacy opportunities. The researchers' balanced view of reading instruction reminds us that even when children become proficient decoders, they still have much to learn about reading. They caution that

> even for beginners, reading should not be thought of simply as a "skill subject." It is difficult to imagine, for instance, that kindergartners could be called literate for their age if they did not know *Goldilocks and the Three Bears* or *Peter Rabbit*. For each age, there are fables, fairy tales, folk tales, classic and modern works of fiction and nonfiction that embody the core of our cultural heritage. (p. 61)

Somehow, BNR provides us with the texture—or sensibility—that reminds us that reading is much more than learning the code. Yet, both phonics and literature study are inseparable if we intend to teach a balanced approach to reading instruction.

CHAPTER 5

Beginning to Read: Thinking and Learning About Print

(Marilyn Jager Adams, 1990a)

Marilyn Jager Adams's research study, *Beginning to Read: Thinking and Learning About Print*, is deemed by many researchers as a "worthy sequel to Chall's [1967] book, *Learning to Read: The Great Debate*" (Seidenberg, 1990, n.p.). In fact, Adams's work was to become the most widely quoted since Chall's, perhaps due to the subsequent and nearly simultaneous publication of *Beginning to Read: Thinking and Learning About Print: A Summary* (1990b)—a more reader friendly and marketable paperback version prepared by Steven A. Stahl, Jean Osborn, and Fran Lehr in collaboration with Adams.

In a historic sense, Adams's (1990a) study was not due so much to economic or military defense concerns as it was to the continuing debate of the reading wars. This time, the debate shifted from phonics versus "whole-word" to phonics versus "whole language." In both instances, phonics is pitted against a meaning-first emphasis (i.e., basal readers [1960s] or authentic literature [1990s]). Whole language, mistakenly thought by reading teachers in the United States to be modeled after the New Zealand "balanced" approach, advocates the use of authentic literature and whole-word instruction over drill and direct, explicit instruction. Most whole language advocates flatly refused to teach phonics in any systematic or routine way. That is not to say that some phonics might not be taught along the way, especially if it happened in the context of a teachable moment.

Adams's (1990a) objective was not to outline a best method of instruction, because surely she had learned from the prior U.S. national research studies that no particular reading method had ever proven more effective than another. Adams does indicate, however, that her own research validates the evidence of the past, and that we now know much more about how beginning readers learn to read. Therefore, her intent was to establish principles and goals that would enable teachers, publishers, and other interested stakeholders to develop a method of instructing children that included a balance of code emphasis and meaning emphasis. This balanced approach would avoid the divisiveness that Chall (1967) had addressed in her study. Unfortunately, this divisiveness continued for more than another decade after Adams's 1990 publication. It peaked in 1994, perhaps, in an inflammatory media report that fourth-grade students in California scored next to the lowest in the nation in reading on the National Assessment of Educational Progress (NAEP), which was an embarrassing showing of this large, prestigious state's educational system. Unfortunately, this low performance in reading was announced shortly after California's Superintendent of Schools, Bill Honig, had declared that the state curriculum had been dedicated to a whole language approach to beginning reading. California's educational system was being castigated for teaching beginning reading using a meaning-emphasis approach while basically ignoring the teaching of phonics. Naturally, these accusations were largely exaggerated, but even Honig admitted that he had allowed the system to wander too far from a code-emphasis approach in favor of whole language, conceding what he believed to be the cause of so many California children failing to read. However, California teacher-author Gail Tompkins (1997) provides a more sensible rationale for California's literacy problems, citing the economic downturn, class sizes of 32–36 students, and a majority of English language learners speaking as many as three different languages in the same classroom.

During the mid-1990s, the California School District, under great political and media pressure, abandoned its support of whole language in favor of a more structured, basal reading program, not too different from what it had left only a few years prior to the sensationalized reporting of that district's poor NAEP reading scores.

To some extent, it appears that the purpose of Adams's research and message offers a solution to the phonics-versus-whole language debate by trying to bring balance and reason to solving this age-old problem caused by the inconsistent nature of the English writing system. In fact, Adams (1990a) states that her goal was to provide guidance in relation to how phonics instruction can be taught efficiently and effectively and, especially, to support the real purpose of learning to read—comprehension. Actually, some whole language teachers in the United States, like their New Zealand counterparts, were successful teaching the code systematically along with connected authentic texts (Clay, 1993; Cowen, 1983). In fact, the ability to teach phonics and literature in a seamless fashion is, in part, what is meant by a "balanced approach to reading." Since 1912, systematic code studies have been shown to outdistance basal readers and whole-word or meaning-first approaches (Anderson, Hiebert, Scott, & Wilkinson, 1985; Bond & Dykstra, 1967; Chall, 1967). Likewise, Adams's (1990a) convergent findings conclude that "Approaches in which systematic code instruction is included along with the reading of meaningful connected text result in superior reading achievement overall, for both low-readiness and better prepared students" (p. 125). Chall's (1967) and Bond and Dykstra's (1967) studies conclude that the two best predictors of beginning reading success are (1) knowledge of the alphabet letters and their names and (2) phonemic awareness (how sounds can be manipulated in words). Adams's research points out that it is not merely letter-naming accuracy that is important, but also the speed and automaticity with which beginning readers can achieve this skill. Anderson et al. (1985) reported very similar findings, writing that "One of the cornerstones of skilled reading is fast, accurate word identification" (p. 36). Adams also emphasizes the necessity of teaching both phonemic awareness and the alphabetic principle, which when linked together, accelerate reading acquisition. Although Adams did not invent or discover the concept of phonemic awareness, a concept that is alluded to in each of the three aforementioned studies (Anderson et al., 1985; Bond & Dykstra, 1967; Chall, 1967), her synthesis of beginning reading research focused on the importance of phonemic awareness as a prerequisite to learning phonics and learning to read. In fact, 1990 may be remembered in the annals of reading research as the year Adams proclaimed phonemic awareness as the basis for learning to read. Adams states that phonemic awareness is the conscious knowledge that spoken language can be manipulated and that this concept is necessary for children to learn to read. It is necessary that beginning readers start learning the alphabetic principle early and to link what they know about segmenting and blending phonemes to letters or graphemes, thereby making letter-sound correspondences. Once children have become consciously aware of phonemic awareness and can link the letters of the alphabet to individual graphemes, they have developed the concepts required for learning phonics, two of the major underpinnings on which reading is ultimately dependent. From 1990 until today, there appears to be no skill other than phonemic awareness that has received greater attention or emphasis based on the number of articles, books, materials, tests, workshops, conference presentations, and curricula changes in early reading instruction.

Of course, the age-old question remains: How do we best teach phonemic awareness? More recent studies accrued since 1990—most notably Ehri, Nunes, Willows, Schuster, Yaghoub-Zadeh, and Shanahan (2001)—point out the amount of time that should be devoted to phonemic awareness is less than 20 hours during an entire school year. Richgels (2001) has even proposed the following five criteria for evaluating the deluge of phonemic awareness materials that were marketed as a result of Adams's highly published research recommendations:

1. A definition of *phoneme* that tells how phonemes work in spoken language;

2. A definition of *awareness* that emphasizes conscious attention;

3. The realization that phonemes are not discrete entities, but rather are categories within which there's much variation;

4. Delineation of the differences among phonological, phonemic, and phonic; and

5. An appreciation of the small, albeit necessary, part that phonemic awareness plays in beginning reading and writing.

Richgels's rationale is that educators must be adequately informed to make appropriate instructional decisions before jumping blindly onto the proverbial phonemic awareness bandwagon. These five factors emphasize how much Adams influenced future research in this area and on classroom instruction changes relative to beginning reading. Adams's synthesis of the available literary research is most impressive because she also reviews the psycholinguistic processes of reading, which provide other converging research evidence from the subdisciplines of psychology, including child development, linguistics, and education. Other major contributions of Adams's (1990b) research include a number of findings and conclusions about beginning reading that resulted in the following recommendations:

- The single most important activity for building the knowledge and skills eventually required for reading appears to be reading aloud to children.
- Faced with an alphabetic script, children's levels of phonemic awareness on entering school may be the single most powerful determinant of their success—or failure—in learning to read.
- Although phonemic awareness is not spontaneously acquired, it can be taught successfully. Furthermore, when reading instruction is methodically coupled with such training, the success rates are dramatic.
- Direct instruction in phonics in early reading acquisition in phonics is necessary.
- Instruction must focus on orthographic regularities of English at the beginning stages.
- The code is not enough, and practice with lots of reading texts is important to develop fluency.
- Automatic processing of word recognition is necessary to develop vocabulary understanding.
- To develop vocabulary understanding practice with authentic, interesting literature is necessary.
- Children must be encouraged to read often and independently to acquire facility and to develop lasting motivation to read for pleasure and information.
- Children must be taught concepts about print very early in their school program, as well as those concepts about words, sentences, and stories.
- Children must develop phonemic awareness and an understanding of the alphabetic principle in order to be successful in

phonics and ultimately to be successful in their acquisition of reading skills and reading for comprehension.

Although Adams's contribution to predictors of reading acquisition is invaluable, she is most supportive of a balanced approach to reading, as the above statements attest. Adams also has added several important refinements to the U.S. studies previously summarized in this book, in which, for example, she declares that to learn how to read, children need to read words quickly, accurately, and effortlessly in order to read with understanding and with skillful comprehension. Adams clearly concludes that phonics instruction is not enough. She advocates instead that children must practice decoding by *seeing and understanding* these newly learned words by reading them in authentic, connected texts. Adams's supportive stance of a balanced reading process is one of seamless integration consisting of a variety of components, or pieces, that fit together and work as one integrated, interdependent system, based on the continuous assessed needs of young readers.

Adams's research conclusions also prompted her to recommend an onset and rime approach, which has several advantages over traditional phonics instruction because

- phonic generalizations are frustratingly unreliable;
- vowel sounds are quite stable in rimes; and
- vowel digraphs are consistent in pronunciation, for example, *ea* as long *e* (except in the rimes –ear [*hear*], –ead [*head*], and –eaf [*deaf*])

Adams also reports that researchers have found that children learn rimes or phonograms, more widely known as word families or spelling patterns, much faster and easier in contrast to learning how to "pronounce vowels using spelling-sound correspondences" (1990a, p. 320) and unreliable phonic generalizations. Adams's research synthesis is one of the first to be critical of the wide use of phonics rules that, in fact, are correct less than half of the time. This inaccurate application of phonic rules, therefore, confuses and frustrates children more often than not while they are learning to apply the skill of phonics while decoding words in sentences. Adams's research also illustrates how much easier it is for children to learn words through sound patterns and rhymes, compared to using phonemics or spelling-sound correspondences to learn complex vowel pronunciations that are so varied and inconsistent. The following examples from Adams illustrate how valuable the teaching of phonograms can be to beginning readers:

- Short vowels and long vowels contained in phonograms are learned equally as well, for instance, s-*ong* or s-*ide*; th-*ong* or thr-*one*;
- Of 286 phonograms, 95% were pronounced the same in every word, reducing confusion in contrast to learning via phonics generalizations;
- Nearly 275 stable rimes are contained in 1,400 common spoken words of primary-level children; and
- Nearly 500 words of high frequency can be derived from the following set of 37 rimes (Wylie & Durrell, as cited in Adams, 1990a), which according to Adams remains quite stable in contrast to the disappointing reliability of phonics rules:

-ack	-all	-ain	-ake	-ale	-ame	-an
-ank	-ap	-ash	-at	-ate	-aw	-ay
-eat	-ell	-est	-ice	-ick	-ide	-ight
-ill	-in	-ine	-ing	-ink	-ip	-ir
-ock	-oke	-op	-ore	-or	-uck	-ug
-ump	-unk	(1990a, p. 321)				

Adams's study also explains the value of invented spelling or temporary spelling as a way for children to discover phonics generalizations. She recommends that having children learn "regular spelling patterns and their phonic significance may be hastened through methodical use of onset and rimes" (1990a, p. 322).

In contrast to the first three national studies discussed in this book, Adams's (1990a) findings seem to more fully recognize the importance of the home and community on beginning reading preparedness, recommending the necessity of such mediated learning opportunities as (a) developing young children's literacy understanding through regular reading aloud, (b) the importance of the spoken word, (c) learning the letters of the alphabet, (d) opportunities to learn how print and words work on the page in a book, and (e) the importance of teaching children nursery rhymes, a prerequisite to learning phonemic awareness and phonics.

For instance, Adams points out how fast the literacy gap can widen even before a child enters school to begin formal reading instruction. For example, Adams once calculated having read aloud more than 1,000 hours to her own child before he reached first grade, and that he continued learning how to read with ease. In contrast, Adams points to research studies showing how children from lower socioeconomic communities are given only a small fraction of that time (26 hours) to listen to parents or siblings read books aloud to them and provide opportunities for them to interact or discuss the pictures or characters in the text. Studies show that this early deprivation will have a dramatically negative impact on these children's ability to profit from initial reading instruction, and, therefore, teacher interventions will need to be intense, skillful, and as Adams states, "there is not a classroom moment to waste" (1990b, p. 48).

Adams's research is based also on models of psycholinguistics that develop an understanding of the reading process by examining and explaining the importance of a reading system that is interconnected by four processors. Adams begins by stating that "Reading depends first and foremost on visual processing" (1990a, p. 158) (letter recognition), and that the four processors engaged in the contexts of literacy must work in a synchronized way like a finely tuned automobile engine (see Appendix A). That is, a good reader must do more than simply decode words. To be an effective reader one also must develop a full understanding of these words, including their spellings, meanings, and pronunciations, and be able to read them with fluency in the various contexts in which they appear. Adams (1990a/1990b) describes a reading system that depicts four key components or processors at work in a synchronized way, which shows how strongly her research supports a balanced approach to reading instruction (see Figure 1):

- The Orthographic Processor is responsible for perceiving the sequences of letters in the text.

FIGURE 1
Modeling the reading system: Four processors

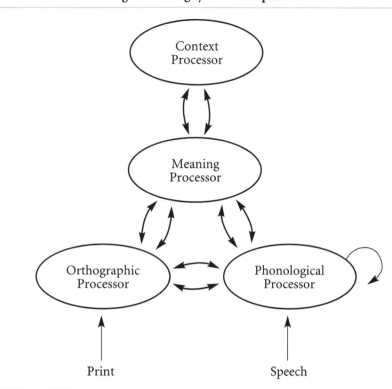

From Adams, M.J. (1990a), p. 158.

- The Phonological Processor is responsible for mapping the letters onto their spoken equivalents.
- The Meaning Processor contains our knowledge of word meanings.
- The Context Processor is in charge of constructing an ongoing understanding of the text. (1990b, p. 21)

Strengths of the Study

More than any of the previous studies discussed in this book, Adams's research takes a broader view of beginning reading by raising and pondering such questions as (a) What is the reading process? (b) If there are four processors integral to the reading system, how do they work independently, interdependently, and as an integrated whole? (c) How are all the pieces that we know about literacy combined to operate in a synchronized and effective way? (d) How do we develop the depth and quality of understanding effective reading instruction to guide what we do as classroom teachers for beginning readers?

By raising such questions and by exploring answers to such broad issues, Adams is one of the first researchers to explain and to provide supporting evidence from a growing body of cross-discipline approaches from many developing fields that include cognitive psychology, developmental psychology, educational psychology, education, linguistics, computer science, and anthropology. This integration of evidence from so many divergent yet related fields provides a stronger perspective on beginning reading instruction as compared to earlier researchers.

Adams is also responsible for embracing a more balanced approach to reading instruction by her expressed desire to put an end to the long and destructive reading wars surrounding phonics instruction that had continued to be counterproductive to solving children's reading problems. The 1990s also ushered in the age of cybernetics and the need for a more advanced literate society. In order to be able to function in a higher order socioeconomic society, young people would be required to be fully educated and prepared to engage in more technologically demanding tasks. By showing that phonics is taught compatibly within a print-rich and authentic-literature-rich environment, Adams seems to have opened the gateway toward a broader acceptance of teaching using a balanced reading approach. Adams endorses Clay's (1993) Reading Recovery program, a balanced approach that promotes diagnostic teaching and uses surveys and running records to assess individual students' letter recognition ability, knowledge of concepts about print, reading for meaning, and writing using invented spelling. Reading Recovery and other intervention programs described by Adams employ balanced literacy to help low-achieving students succeed. These intervention programs include a thorough appreciation of phonics, coordinated with a facility and knowledge about language and text (use of emergent leveled readers); phonological awareness and letter recognition; spelling patterns; and spelling-sound relations. Adams also stresses that these skills need to be developed in a balanced way that incorporates authentic reading and writing, and that children should be engaged in discussions about the form, function, and meaning of these texts. Reading for meaning is valued highly by Adams, and according to Pearson (2001), Adams's underlying message is "The goal of all instruction—be it phonics, vocabulary, comprehension, studying, thinking, or mathematical problem solving—ought to be to promote cognitive clarity for students" (p. viii).

Limitations of the Study

Dorothy Strickland and Bernice Cullinan (1990), advisory board members for Adams's study, express their concerns in the afterword of *Beginning to Read* that it does not include a sufficient amount of research evidence related to developmental views of language and literacy learning. I agree with Strickland and Cullinan, who share the view that Adams's study, particularly the concluding chapter, gives practitioners the impression that only direct and explicit teaching can be used effectively to teach phonics and related skills to beginning readers. As pointed out earlier in this chapter, Adams's support for a more balanced and developmental approach is evident throughout her study. For instance, Strickland and Cullinan are highly critical of Adams's frequent references to a readiness approach to beginning reading rather than an emergent reader's approach, which they believe changes the researcher's perspective to being directive rather than to being responsive and reflective. Similarly, these critics show how Adams appears to undervalue beginning readers' interest in self-discovery, even though the study does describe how the use of invented spelling is one way that children discover phonics principles on their own. Strickland and Cullinan also believe that Adams places too much emphasis on an early prescriptive, scope-and-sequence approach to phonics rather than using a more responsive, reflective, or embedded phonics approach that might be used with better lasting effects.

On the other hand, Strickland and Cullinan praise Adams for writing with style and grace while handling an overwhelming body of literacy research data. Nevertheless, this afterword is quite direct in expressing concerns about the limitations of the study, but is positive overall, embracing Adams's research evidence that, in general, supports a whole language and integrated language arts approach. They conclude by stating that "Adams moves us closer to our goal of ending the phonics debate by leading us to ask not if, but how and when, spelling-sound information is made available to learners" (1990a, p. 433).

From another very important historical perspective, the 1990s saw a major demographic shift in dominance particularly with regard to cultural and linguistic populations entering U.S. schools. Although Adams's research does report a few such studies of low-socioeconomic, urban populations investigating parent and community responsibility for providing a literate environment for preschool children—similar to Chall's and Bond and Dykstra's studies conducted in 1967—none of the studies provide enough direction in meeting the dire needs of this burgeoning population of struggling readers.

Similarly, Adams's study provides very little information with regard to the widespread failure of basic skills programs or other preventive programs, other than Reading Recovery and the Follow Through Studies (Stebbins, St. Pierre, Proper, Anderson, & Cerva, 1977) conducted in the 1970s, to determine which models succeed with preschool disadvantaged children. She concludes that most programs were unsuccessful from a number of research and related practical perspectives to be considered seriously, because gains that were made disappeared when children left the program. In fact, during the 1980s and 1990s, a number of research studies frequently reported on the widening literacy gaps and poor achievement of African American and Latino students compared to Caucasian and Asian students. Although most remedial programs at this time were being implemented after grades 2 and 3, Adams should have investigated this growing problem, which continues to manifest itself to this day. One can only wonder about the outcome if intervention programs such as Reading Recovery—an effective program introduced in grade one—were introduced earlier in kindergarten or preschool.

Similarly, the vast numbers of children entering the schools during the 1980s speaking languages other than English continue to increase and to be cause for alarm today. Therefore, it is rather inexplicable as to why the existing research relative to English language learners was not synthesized as part of Adams's study, especially because so many other studies from a variety of cross disciplines were included.

Nevertheless, the limitation attributed to Adams's research report is quite negligible and, like Chall's (1967) seminal study, continues to serve today as a classic reading research study. In fact, as previously mentioned, Strickland and Cullinan's (1990) minority report ends quite positively, acknowledging that "Adams's study moves us closer to our goal of ending the phonics debate" (p. 432). It is my opinion that a noticeable change occurred shortly after Adams's book appeared, and the phonics debate seems to have abated ever since.

CHAPTER 6

Preventing Reading Difficulties in Young Children

(Catherine E. Snow, M. Susan Burns,
& Peg Griffin, 1998)

In the late 1990s, it was dramatically clear that the next generation would be living in a vastly changed technological society. This new society would be creating greater demands for higher literacy globally, particularly in the United States where the entire democratic population is expected to be contributing literate citizens. Nowhere else in the world is there such a high degree of expectation. The realization now is that young citizens not only will need to possess a modicum of basic skills proficiency, but also they will need to comprehend at higher levels than ever before to compete in a rapidly changing and challenging technological workplace. It is this concern that led to the major U.S. national literacy report, *Preventing Reading Difficulties in Young Children* (PRD) (Snow, Burns, & Griffin, 1998), sponsored by the U.S. Department of Education and National Academy of Sciences.

The National Academy of Sciences was commissioned to establish a committee charged with conducting a study to determine effective interventions for young children at risk of learning how to read. Three goals directed the study: (1) to create a comprehensive, diverse research base; (2) to translate and disseminate the findings and recommendations to parents, to the educational community, and to publishers; and (3) to engage targeted audiences in order to convey this advice. These goals, though far-reaching and ambitious, are more community-action-based than any of the previous studies presented in this book. PRD addresses education for preservice and inservice teachers, preschool educators, and others working with young children. The scope and aim of the study is intent on influencing major stakeholders in the literacy arena, including federal, state, and local government policies. Consequently, nursery school, preschool, and, eventually, elementary school personnel will be able to use the research from PRD to implement best practices to prevent reading difficulties for young at-risk children. Snow, Burns, and Griffin provide the following list of initial reading instruction findings requiring that children

- use reading to obtain meaning from print,
- have frequent and intensive opportunities to read,
- be exposed to frequent, regular spelling-sound relationships,
- learn about the nature of the alphabetic writing system, and
- understand the structure of spoken words. (1998, p. 3)

The study indicates that progress in learning to read English (or any alphabetic language) beyond the initial level depends on

- having a working understanding of how sounds are represented alphabetically,
- sufficient practice in reading to achieve fluency with different kinds of texts,
- sufficient background knowledge and vocabulary to render written texts meaningful and interesting,
- control over procedures for monitoring comprehension and repairing misunderstandings, and
- continued interest and motivation to read for a variety of purposes. (1998, pp. 3–4)

This list of recommendations is authoritative, but like most of the other studies stops short of recommending specific instructional approaches, materials, or texts. Nevertheless, PRD does provide a thorough and comprehensive analysis of findings for each of these instructional and resource areas from which the reader can review and select. The above list also mirrors some of the most basic elements of a balanced, comprehensive, or integrated approach to a sound reading program. However, Snow, Burns, and Griffin seem to deny that their report endorses a balanced reading approach. In fact, the researchers include a disclaimer in "Addition to the Preface" of

PRD (third printing) by restating their core message of reading instruction: "That reading instruction integrate attention to the alphabetic principle with attention to the construction of meaning and opportunities to develop fluency" (1998, p. vii). Their purpose for writing this is to stress the committee's position so as not to interpret an endorsement of "balance" to mean "some phonics and some whole language" (p. vii), a position also endorsed by the editors. Snow, Burns, and Griffin go on to define what most readers will, perhaps, consider to be PRD's classic definition of "balanced reading," or, at the very least, the "balanced-integration" approach to reading instruction:

> "Balance" could mean splitting one's time evenly across activities designed to practice the alphabetic principle and activities designed to support comprehension. "Integration" means precisely that the opportunities to learn these two aspects of skilled reading should be going on at the same time, in the context of the same activities, and that the choice of instructional activities should be part of an overall, coherent approach to supporting literacy development, not a haphazard selection from unrelated, though varied, activities. (1998, p. viii)

PRD's first- through third-grade recommendations are aimed at preventing reading difficulties for young children who are at risk, but the researchers conclude that these components are necessary criteria for developing all children's literacy development. In fact, the study points out that all children require exemplary instruction from knowledgeable and skillful teachers. The recommended curricula, therefore, include the following essential components:

Beginning Readers

- Use explicit instruction and practice in phonemic awareness to help children develop spelling-sound correspondences, learn common spelling conventions to identify unfamiliar words, build "sight" recognition of high-frequency words, and improve reading fluency through practice with engaging texts at a child's independent reading level.
- Encourage children as soon as possible to use invented spelling to practice writing letters and parts of words and to use words to begin writing sentences.

- Use writing regularly and frequently to develop ease, familiarity, and comfort in this area.

Research recognizes the reciprocal value of invented spelling in developing phonemic awareness and phonic skills in beginning readers. As children develop fluency in these areas they should be taught to use spelling patterns as a vehicle to learn conventional spelling for final writing products.

Second Grade and Up

- Encourage independent reading, sounding out unfamiliar words encountered in reading meaningful texts, and only using context and illustrations to monitor word recognition.
- Use continuous classroom assessment and timely intervention to monitor student development or delay in word-recognition accuracy and reading fluency.

All Primary Levels

- Promote, encourage, and become active participants in specific comprehension strategies such as summarizing the main idea, predicting events and outcomes, drawing inferences and monitoring for meaning through explicit instruction, and actively building linguistic and conceptual knowledge through discourse and analysis of a variety of texts.
- Provide time, materials, and resources with two goals: (1) to enable children to read engaging, enjoyable, well-written texts daily and frequently at their independent level (never at their frustration level) and (2) to support daily assisted or guided reading and rereading of texts at the child's instructional level to promote continuous reading progress and to advance his or her literacy achievement.
- Foster independent reading outside the school by (1) establishing at-home reading assignments, (2) creating and monitoring summer reading lists, and (3) engaging parents, community, and public librarians in this shared goal.

PRD's research basically supports the findings of its predecessors discussed in this book; however, it places greater importance on phonological awareness and the need to provide direct instruction in this area. The study also establishes guidelines for literacy instruction starting as early as the preschool level and kindergarten. In contrast to its predecessors, PRD is the first report to promote such an extensive list of guidelines in literacy instruction at this early level. For example the report points out that some children enter kindergarten

> having already become aware of the existence of syllables, onsets and rimes, and even phonological segments. Research indicates that the latter are very likely to turn out to be successful readers.... Many can and do begin to attain this sensitivity during the kindergarten year and respond successfully once formal reading initiation begins. (1998, p. 185)

PRD also concludes that fostering literacy in the kindergarten classroom depends on two goals: (1) "that children leave kindergarten familiar with the structural elements and organization of print; ...they should also have some basic phonemic awareness...," and (2) "to establish perspectives and attitudes on which learning about and from print depend..." (1998, p. 179). PRD, like the other studies, is supportive of the tenets of a balanced approach to reading instruction. Pearson's (1999) estimate of the study's significance is that "[PRD] made a strong case for the position that authenticity of task and text need not stand in opposition to explicit instruction in important skills and strategies" (p. 244).

PRD devotes chapters 4 and 8 to the predictors of individual and group risk factors, many of which relate to children from low-socioeconomic levels, teaching reading to language minority children, and some predictable causes of disparity in reading. In chapter 4, it is pointed out that there are many causal problems that can predict reading failure, but the report also indicates that "no single risk factor" (1998, p. 131) can be used for predicting reading difficulties. However, when multiple or a combination of measures are used, it is possible to predict reading problems. Some of these individual risk factors for students are summarized as follows:

1. Parents have histories of reading difficulty;
2. Students have less knowledge and literacy skills acquired during preschool years due to the home environment or inherent cognitive limitations;

3. Students lack phonological awareness, confrontational naming, sentence/story recall, and general language ability;

4. Students are diagnosed with specific language impairment;

5. Students have a hearing impairment; and

6. Students have primary medical diagnosis that impedes reading as a secondary symptom.

PRD recommends that the best course of action in dealing with the above risk factors is to provide early intervention as soon as possible from birth to preschool. Kindergarten screening using multiple measures also can predict children at risk, and early classroom intervention measures can be implemented successfully. In cases in which large populations are at risk, best practice interventions might need to be applied schoolwide.

Perhaps, PRD's most controversial recommendation relates to teaching non–English-speaking children. Research finds that, "hurrying young non–English-speaking children into reading in English without ensuring adequate preparation is counterproductive" (1998, p. 246). PRD recommends, therefore, that, "To the extent possible, non–English-speaking children should have opportunities to develop literacy skills in their home language as well as in English" (1998, p. 246). In brief, it is clear that a great deal of research is needed in all the special population areas, most noticeably in teaching English language learners to be successful readers of English. Perhaps more cross-disciplinary research and dialogues between world-language teachers and reading teachers would be helpful in speeding up the process in closing the literacy gap for children who are new to reading and writing in English.

Strengths of the Study

Although some of the studies reported earlier in this book address diversity issues related to reading instruction and achievement among minority groups of African American and Latino children, English language learners, and children with specific reading disabilities and other handicapping conditions, only PRD provides a modicum of recommendations for improving instruction in this important area. These recommendations are based on conclusions drawn from these researchers' studies of the problems underlying the causes of reading difficulties that continue to exist disproportionately within these populations. It is especially troubling, however, that so few of the published research studies have addressed this constant and growing concern in a comprehensive, meaningful way.

According to Bowler (2000), "NAEP results, [show] the disparity between black and white performance, which had narrowed in the 1980s widened in the 1990s for 13- and-17-year olds across the nation—remained steady or dropped last year" (p. 2b). Bowler also reports that "Only in 1971, the first year in which NAEP measured reading, was there a wider point spread between black and white 9-year-olds according to the study" (p. 2b), and that reading scores for Hispanic children are shown to be even lower.

PRD gives us a balanced reading view of how young struggling readers learn to read. We find out early in this study that all children, whether they are good readers, struggling readers, readers with special needs, or readers who come from poor urban areas with low-socioeconomic home environments, they basically learn best in classrooms that use a balanced reading program. PRD, in providing the predictors of success and the failures of reading, provides a number of highly researched correlates that include perceptual, linguistic, cognitive, environmental, and social causalities. The study examines instructional strategies while providing benchmarks for each primary grade level beginning as early as kindergarten through grade 3. PRD, for the first time, takes a definitive stance, giving a strong endorsement of an early formal reading instruction program for kindergarten students. PRD also reports the research findings from a number of literacy programs that seem to deal effectively with at-risk struggling readers from multicultural, low-socioeconomic environments.

According to Pearson (1999), PRD is a "must-read" book for preservice and inservice teachers and reading teachers because the study provides valid, important information about

- research on the process of reading acquisition;
- roadblocks that prevent children from reading; and

- instructional strategies and tools available for preventing and correcting reading problems.

Furthermore, PRD is also one of the first studies to report from several important areas of research, including cognitive psychology, language development, special education, medicine, and literacy education (Pearson, 1999), while reporting the most up-to-date available reading research on at-risk, struggling readers, including

- the nature and etiology of reading difficulties,
- evaluation of reading interventions, and
- evaluation of cognitive and linguistic development of preschool emergent readers to promote language development and concepts about print.

PRD seems to provide one of the strongest cases for a balanced approach to reading instruction even though its findings converge with each of its four antecedent research studies (that appear in this book) calling for an early code emphasis, but PRD suggests that a balanced approach also must emphasize meaning. Like the other reported studies, PRD agrees that early attention to the alphabetic principle is necessary, but it also supports wide reading, wide writing, and attention to specific reading comprehension strategies. Finally, the report also stresses the importance of teaching children to self-monitor their reading through cross-checking and self-correction, which develop largely through the use of the running record and other informal, continuous early assessment procedures.

Limitations of the Study

Although PRD did not include a minority report written by a committee member, it is likely that the very issues critiqued by Chall (1985) with regard to *Becoming a Nation of Readers* or that some of the nagging, controversial issues addressed by Strickland and Cullinan in *Beginning to Read* are just as relevant to *Preventing Reading Disabilities in Young Children*. Although PRD does not address specific issues such as dyslexia or adult literacy to any major extent—two key omissions pointed out in Chall's afterword to *Becoming a Nation of Readers*—PRD probably does the best job of addressing related concerns of specific learning disabilities that affect reading acquisition and is also one of the few studies that addresses diversity and related literacy disparity issues.

Like the studies preceding it, PRD also does not take advantage of ethnographic, qualitative research to support, or at least provide, other instructional perspectives in addressing phonics. Phonics is now more or less accepted by most literacy research experts and classroom teachers and other reading practitioners; nevertheless, the unresolved questions still being debated are to what degree, with what amount of emphasis, using what kinds of support materials, and within which reading contexts is phonics best taught? Like the other studies, these questions are not answered with any degree of certainty in PRD, and these questions are not dealt with using research designs that might be capable of revealing how children learn best. Anderson and his associates (1985), at the end of their study, seem to discover how to resolve some of these research design issues, and, although quoted earlier, it bears repeating in this context: "America will become a nation of readers when verified practices of the best teachers in the best schools can be introduced throughout the country" (p. 120).

Pearson (1999) takes a serious, philosophical view of PRD and its importance, stating,

> Never have we, as a profession, had greater cause to take this professional responsibility seriously. If professional groups wish to retain the privileges of teacher prerogative and choice that we value so dearly, then the price we must pay is constant attention to new knowledge as a vehicle for fine-tuning our individual and collective views of best practice [or]...we will find ourselves victims of the most onerous of legislative mandates. (p. 245)

CHAPTER 7

Report of the National Reading Panel: Teaching Children to Read: An Evidence-Based Assessment of the Scientific Research Literature on Reading and Its Implications for Reading Instruction

(National Institute of Child Health and Human Development, 2000)

The introduction to the *Report of the National Reading Panel: Teaching Children to Read* (NRP) states that it took into account the foundational work of *Preventing Reading Difficulties in Young Children* (PRD) (Snow, Burns, & Griffin, 1998). The NRP report refers to PRD as a "consensus document" that did not address how to teach reading skills or recommend "what methods, materials or approaches to use with students of varying abilities" (p. 1-1). In lieu of the strong effort made by the National Research Council to disseminate the highly acclaimed PRD published just in 1998, the call for this new study seems somewhat unusual.

Reading became an important political issue during the 1990s, so much so that U.S. congressman William Goodling of Pennsylvania introduced the Reading Excellence Act (H.B. 2416) to the U.S. House of Representatives on November 7, 1997, which marked the beginning of legislation focused on reading. Some critics, including many reading professionals, found that the original version of the bill was objectionable for a number of reasons, including its definition of reading, its definition of research, and the constitution of the panel that would evaluate and be responsible for recommending future funding (Roller, 2000). Not only had most state governments begun to establish state literacy standards and high-stakes testing during the 1990s, but now the federal government and legislators began introducing and passing bills on important literacy legislation of which it would soon take charge, making educational decisions and even controlling the funding of major sources of grant allocations for reading and literacy development. What is even more alarming is that just prior to the establishment of the National Reading Panel (NRP) in 1997, one of the largest reading/literacy associations in the world—the International Reading Association (IRA)—seemed to have been deliberately left out of the decision-making process. However, it was at this juncture that the Association decided that it had to play an important part in this political process. IRA would have a voice in the establishment of future policy related to the Reading Excellence Act and to all future legislation related to the future development of reading. In fact, IRA and the National Council of Teachers of English (NCTE) worked with Senator Jim Jeffords of Vermont to gain his support in introducing an amended version of the Reading Excellence Act (Jeffords Amendment No. 3740, Senate, October 6, 1998) that would influence the redefining of reading and research that was, according to Cathy Roller (2000), "far more inclusive and more representative of our understanding of the complexity of the reading process and the extent to which prior knowledge, comprehension, and motivation are important components" (p. 631).

Of course, literacy continued to be a hot media issue throughout the last half of the 1990s and into the 21st century and included issues such as whole language versus phonics, high-stakes testing, and state literacy standards established across the United States. Not only was legislation in reading being passed statewide and nationally, but reading would later become a key campaign issue raised by presidential candidates Al Gore and George W. Bush. Consequently, in 1997 the U.S. Congress asked that a national panel of reading scientists in reading research and other literacy experts be formed to assess the status of research knowledge in reading, and it charged a prominent group of panel members to report whether or not the literacy research results indicated a "readiness of application in the classroom" (p. 1-1).

Five committees or subgroups were formed from this 14-member panel to research five literacy areas. The NRP adopted the following five key topics to be studied and reported:

- Alphabetics—
  - Phonemic Awareness Instruction
  - Phonics Instruction
- Fluency
- Comprehension—
  - Vocabulary Instruction
  - Text Comprehension Instruction
  - Teacher Preparation and Comprehension Strategies Instruction
- Teacher Education and Reading Instruction
- Computer Technology and Reading Instruction (2000, p. 1-2)

In order to meet the charge of the U.S. Congress to identify "instructional reading approaches and [to determine] their readiness for use in the classroom" (p. 1-3), the following six questions guided the NRP researchers in their study. (Each question was followed by the question, "If so, how is this instruction best provided?")

1. Does instruction in phonemic awareness improve reading?
2. Does phonics instruction improve reading achievement?
3. Does guided repeated oral reading instruction improve fluency and reading comprehension?
4. Does vocabulary instruction improve reading achievement?
5. Does comprehension strategy instruction improve reading?
6. Do programs that increase the amount of children's independent reading improve reading achievement and motivation? (p. 1-3)

These questions are quite central to the reading process as discussed in the research of the last 30 years. Although, as we have seen, not everyone views these issues quite the same way, it is evident that there is a growing body of research that is consistently convergent. At the core of early reading instruction, consensus on at least these basic questions might create the balance and common ground the reading profession needs at this crucial time. Although these are not necessarily the only or best questions that need to be resolved, these questions do address similar literacy issues that have been researched diligently over the past decades, and with similar results.

Highlights of the Report

The NRP report is certainly well organized. The research methodology appears to be solid and scholarly and to have been carefully scrutinized by an expert panel of notable researchers. To assist laypeople, business leaders, politicians, and other interested members of the educational community, an executive summary is provided as an introduction to each of the five key topics in the study. An executive summary also precedes the first chapter, describing how each major reading instructional area was studied; the research designs employed; the methodology used to reach conclusions and findings; and, ultimately, the recommendations for reading instruction implementation. This chapter synthesizes the research of the Panel's report, which is also available at the NRP website (http://www.nationalread ingpanel.org). Highlights of the report and conclusions also will be synthesized and presented from the five key topic areas discussed earlier, with an emphasis on the instructional findings in the three major areas of alphabetics, fluency, and comprehension.

Alphabetics

Phonemic Awareness Instruction. NRP researchers studied phonemic awareness in six distinct areas: (1) isolation, (2) identity, (3) categorization, (4) blending, (5) segmentation, and (6) deletion. The study concluded that phonemic awareness methods in each of these six areas are currently available for use in classrooms and are highly recommended. Because the structure of English spelling is alphabetic, it is extremely important for beginning readers to discover and develop phonemic units, but to do so requires direct instruction in the manipulation of sounds and letters in individual words. Such instruction should be addressed playfully in a game-like manner that is developmentally appropriate. The NRP research also found that the use of developmentally appropriate computer software to teach phonemic awareness works quite effectively.

The researchers found that phonemic awareness instruction helped all children—kindergarten through grade 6—to improve in reading, including at-risk students, disabled readers, children of various socioeconomic levels, and English language learners. Phonemic awareness instruction also works effectively with most kindergartners, especially those who are nonreaders or those who are in remedial settings. The NRP research showed that best results were obtained when training sessions lasted less than 20 hours (5–18 hours are recommended), for 25 minutes or less at one time, and in small groups. Instruction in phonemic awareness was found to help children learn to spell, although this approach was not as effective when used with disabled readers. The Panel's findings indicated that students need differing amounts of time and levels of instruction in this area; therefore, assessment prior to instruction is required.

The NRP researchers conclude that phonemic awareness "does not constitute a complete reading program" (p. 2-5). Furthermore, phonemic awareness instruction does not guarantee that all students will enjoy reading success. Rather, lasting achievement will depend on the comprehensiveness of the student's literacy program. Children also must have the opportunity to practice newly acquired phonemic skills by reading words in connected text to develop ease of recognition and reading fluency.

Phonics Instruction. Although the NRP's findings are similar to the studies previously reviewed in this book, there is no evidence that points to one method being more effective than others. The striking difference in this report, however, is that it concludes that phonics instruction is most effective when introduced as early as kindergarten:

> The conclusion drawn is that phonics instruction produces the biggest impact on growth in reading when it begins in kindergarten or 1st grade before children have learned to read independently. These results indicate clearly that systematic phonics instruction in kindergarten and 1st grade is highly beneficial and that children at these developmental levels are quite capable of learning phonemic and phonics concepts. (2000, p. 2-93)

Of course, the NRP report also cautions that instruction for kindergartners must be developmentally appropriate and include building a "foundational knowledge involving letters and phonemic awareness" (p. 2-93).

In *Becoming a Nation of Readers* (Anderson et al., 1985) and in *Beginning to Read* (Adams, 1990a), the authors similarly point out that teaching phonemic awareness can prove quite effective with children as early as preschool and kindergarten, whereas prior research seemed to question how early children should be exposed to formal reading instruction. Current studies definitely favor teaching phonemic awareness and other literacy readiness skills in kindergarten, including developing emergent reading and writing skills.

The NRP report goes on to say that phonics instruction proved to be successful with all first-grade children, including those diagnosed as potentially at risk or as low-achieving readers. It is interesting to note, however, that phonics instruction failed to maintain this significance with low achievers in grades 2 though 6, and as a result of this finding, the NRP recommends that further research is needed. One could conjecture whether an onset and rime approach might be better suited for this purpose, because Adams's (1990a) research found that other phonic approaches were not as effective with older, struggling readers. Furthermore, Anderson et al. (1985) recommended that formal phonics instruction should not be taught beyond second grade. The NRP (2000) concluded that a systematic phonics approach outdistanced nonsystematic and nonphonics programs, including "basal programs, whole language approaches, and whole-word programs" (p. 2-95).

The NRP also falls very much on the side of a balanced reading approach, stating that "systematic phonics instruction should be integrated with other reading instruction to create a *balanced reading program* [author's emphasis]" (p. 2-97). To this end, the report points out that phonics should not "become the dominant component" (p. 2-97) by overshadowing the child's interest and time devoted to reading books. Rather, it is the comprehensiveness and integration of other components of the reading process that eventually help make the child a successful reader.

Fluency

Although fluency is discussed in all the studies previously reviewed in this book, the NRP report provides the most comprehensive findings for this often overlooked but essential component of reading. The study points out that fluency can refer to the speed or automaticity of word recognition as well as the speed at which children can read text orally or silently. The study also points out that fluency of reading is highly correlated with improved comprehension, and that fluency is taught best through guided interaction with direct feedback provided by a teacher or a knowledgeable facilitator.

However, studies related to independent classroom reading practices such as Sustained Silent Reading (SSR) and Drop Everything And Read (DEAR) showed no appreciable improvement in comprehension (NICHD, 2000). Further studies are needed to investigate more thoroughly these in-class reading approaches that are widely used and favored by teachers and students alike. Recent successful instructional approaches used to influence fluency and comprehension improvement might suggest that parallel studies be used to investigate future recreational reading modified approaches (Block & Mangieri, 2002). Consequently, the use of more transactional reading opportunities for children (Rosenblatt, cited in Cowen, 1999/2000) to interact and to discuss their independent reading experiences with their peers might be beneficial. Transactional, peer-directed discussion groups, and literature circles, for example, seem to be effective in motivating children to read for joy and aesthetic pleasure while developing their comprehension and life-long reading skills in non-threatening classrooms. In contrast to the NRP conclusions, Block and Mangieri's study on recreational reading shows

> students who spent more time in recreational reading activities (a) scored higher on comprehension tests in grades 2, 4, 8, and 12; (b) had significantly higher grade point averages; and (c) developed more sophisticated writing styles than peers who did not engage in recreational reading. (2002, pp. 572–573)

To develop fluency and speed of reading, the NRP recommends instructing children to read the punctuation or to read in thought groups. Developing fluency will help readers read faster with greater understanding; readers who are not fluent tend to read in an irregular cadence, in a staccato or stuttering fashion. Consequently, they tend to perseverate more on individual letters, sounds, or words and not on the phrases or clauses that connect meaning readily. Teachers should monitor student progress in word recognition and text fluency by employing informal reading inventories and running records (Clay, 1993). The use of such informal assessments will enable teachers to provide necessary immediate feedback and guidance to help individual students progress in this critical area.

The NRP's findings have encouraged the recommendation of two approaches for developing fluency: repeated reading and guided repeated oral reading. These two approaches are shown to help students read faster, more accurately, and with greater expression. Students, under the watchful eye of a teacher, peer, tutor, or aided by an audiotape recorder, read passages until they feel proficient enough to read the text aloud, demonstrating their improved accuracy, speed, and fluency. These fluency activities are best conducted as a one-on-one activity and need to be practiced during SSR to achieve automaticity or speed and natural application of the skill.

In contrast, the NRP found that oral fluency does not improve when teachers use the round-robin approach, that is, having students take turns reading aloud in small or large groups with little or no individual guidance. Findings regarding the use of the round-robin approach indicate that such procedures are "boring, anxiety provoking, disruptive of fluency, and wasteful of instructional time" (Stallings, as cited in NICHD, 2000, p. 3-11). Some other recommended techniques to improve fluency according to the NRP report include "repeated reading, neurological impress, radio reading, paired reading, and a variety of other similar procedures" (p. 3-11) such as Readers Theatre.

In brief, the NRP's findings with regard to fluency are very encouraging in that teacher concentration in developing this skill with all students—normal, at-risk, low-achieving, ESL, and disabled students— may increase their overall reading comprehension achievement.

Comprehension

NRP research findings indicate that reading comprehension development is largely dependent on three important dominant themes emerging from the study: (1) vocabulary instruction development, (2) direct teaching of specific text comprehension strategies, and (3) teacher preparation and reading instruction. These three important concomitant areas are illustrated as follows:

Vocabulary Instruction. The NRP findings indicate that "reading vocabulary is crucial to the comprehension processes of a skilled reader" (p. 4-3). As a result of this important research conclusion, five recommended methods of teaching vocabulary have been identified:

1. Explicit Instruction: Students are given definitions or other attributes of words to be learned.
2. Implicit Instruction: Students are exposed to words or given opportunities to do a great deal of reading.
3. Multimedia Methods: Vocabulary is taught by going beyond text to include other media such as graphic representations, hypertext, or American Sign Language that uses a haptic medium.
4. Capacity Methods: Practice is emphasized to increase capacity through making reading automatic.
5. Association Methods: Learners are encouraged to draw connections between what they do know and words they encounter that they do not know. (p. 4-3)

The following are implications for increased reading comprehension achievement concluded by NRP researchers:

• Direct instruction of vocabulary is required for specific text.
• Repetition and multiple exposure to vocabulary in context are important.
• Vocabulary learned in the various content areas should be useful in many contexts, learning to deal with specific reading matter in content areas.
• Computer vocabulary instruction shows positive learning gains over traditional methods; therefore, it should be used advantageously.
• Preinstruction of vocabulary words prior to reading can facilitate both vocabulary acquisition and comprehension.

Specific Reading Comprehension Instruction and Teacher Preparation. The following NRP findings show eight specific comprehension strategies that appear to be effective for classroom instructional use. These strategies can be implemented effectively when teachers receive appropriate inservice training in the metacognitive areas.

1. Comprehension self-monitoring
2. Cooperative and peer learning through context reading strategies
3. Graphic and semantic organizers to aid word and text understanding
4. Story structure scaffolding strategies
5. Question answering and feedback response
6. Reader questioning generated about text
7. Reader summarization of main ideas
8. Teaching about multiple-strategies

The NRP finds that when teachers learn how to teach these specific strategies effectively, "their students learn them and improve their reading comprehension" (p. 4-6). Furthermore, the report states, "this development [is] the most important finding of the Panel's review because it moves from the laboratory to the classroom and prepares teachers to teach strategies in ways that are effective and natural" (p. 46). In short, staff development for teachers to learn how to teach specific comprehension and multiple-strategies is critical, particularly because the Panel's research concludes that "these strategies yield increases in measures of near transfer such as recall, question answering and generation, and summarization of texts. These comprehension strategies, when used in combination, show general gains on standardized comprehension texts" (p. 4-6).

Teacher Education and Reading Instruction

The NRP's conclusions drawn from its analysis of teacher professional development and reading instruction show that appropriate teacher education "does produce higher achievement in students" (p. 5-2).

However, the report goes on to explain that not enough experimental studies related to preservice and inservice education in reading instruction exist, thereby, not allowing the NRP to make specific recommendations for improving this often neglected, yet critical, area of teacher education and its impact on student literacy achievement. The NRP outlines the following issues that still need to be resolved:

- Determining an optimal combination of preservice and inservice experiences
- Determining the effects of preservice experience on inservice performance
- Determining optimal length of pre- and inservice education
- Assessing effectiveness of teacher education and professional development
- Ensuring long-term implementation of new methods and student achievement
- Addressing the gap of knowledge related to the relationship between development of standards and teacher education and professional development

Computer Technology and Reading Instruction

Despite the reported interest in technology and computer use in education and in reading instruction, there are so few experimental research studies available that the NRP could not make specific related instructional recommendations in this critical area. Instead, the Panel reports that future studies related to computer technology and reading instruction are vitally needed. A number of speculative reasons for this dearth of experimental research are offered, including (a) the need to clear up existing problems in reading instruction before addressing technology, (b) the lack of sophisticated software to address reading instruction, (c) the lack of speech recognition in computers until recently, (d) the lack of text sophistication until recently, and (e) the high cost factor. Other inhibitors not mentioned by the Panel are (a) few elementary schools were completely wired for technology until recently, (b) teachers were not well trained in computer usage, and (c) a great deal of resistance to the use of technology in primary classrooms still exists.

Although the number of computer technology research studies was too few to draw substantial conclusions, the Panel did indicate that a number of areas show promise including (a) the use of word processing for writing, (b) the potential use of hypertext for teaching visual comprehension skills, (c) the potential use of interactive software, (d) the recent interest in the Internet, (e) the use of multimedia projects, and (f) the addition of speech to print on computers. All of these technical advances should produce future interest in technological and computer use; hence, the Panel recommends that more conclusive studies are needed. *Preventing Reading Difficulties in Young Children* (1998) does report a number of computer software programs that are very beneficial in teaching vocabulary and phonemic awareness skills. It also points out that more comprehensive literacy software programs exist and, although expensive, hold great promise, for instance, IBM's early innovative program Writing to Read and Pearson Education's Waterford Early Reading Program. Other technology-based programs cited in the research report include Foundations in Learning by Breakthrough and Little Planet Literacy Series by Young Children's Literacy Project.

Strengths of the Study

The NRP report is a well-written, organized, and carefully presented study that reports using systematic, quantitative, and qualitative research methodology. However, as will be discussed in the next section, very little, if any, qualitative research methodology was used to balance this investigation. Also, even though Adams's (1990a) study brought phonemic awareness to the forefront of literacy research and beginning reading instruction, a significant strength of the NRP report is that in accordance with one of its major objectives it has been disseminated widely. In a subsequent report—a kind of teachers' digest summary—*Put Reading First: The Research Building Blocks for Teaching Children to Read* (Armbruster, Lehr, & Osborn, 2001) clearly defines *phonemic awareness* and *phonics* so that the two similar and often-confused terms are readily understood by practitioners:

Phonics is the understanding that there is a predictable relationship between phonemes (the sounds of *spoken* language) and graphemes (the letters and spellings that represent those sounds in *written* language).

Phonemic awareness is the ability to hear, identify, and manipulate the individual sounds—phonemes—in spoken words. (p. 4)

Furthermore, to make phonemic awareness operational on a conscious level, teachers must teach children this concept directly, but playfully, through chanting, rhyming, and segmenting and joining together or blending these sounds. It is also made clear to teachers that children must learn that written spellings and the letters of the alphabet represent spoken sounds that can be read. Once children can accomplish this fundamental task, they can be taught to identify words and new vocabulary automatically. As children learn to identify words with automaticity, they are able to concentrate on reading words with ease and to read them in sentences with greater fluency. By developing fluency, the child's ability to read with comprehension grows, as does the child's reading enjoyment and motivation to continue reading for pleasure and for learning.

The NRP shows the relationship of how children's reading comprehension is developed as they build their vocabulary knowledge and fluency of reading. The study shows how fluency can be developed through repeated readings provided that children receive teacher feedback and encouragement. Fluency also is taught by helping children learn the value and importance of punctuation as it relates to reading for meaning. The NRP report further identifies specific text comprehension skills that enable students to develop higher order thinking skills. Therefore, the study shows how the integration and comprehensive approaches to literacy enable children to develop reading for learning. The process is established, however, not as discrete steps but as an integrated approach and a balance of all the following skills:

- phonemic awareness instruction
- phonics instruction
- fluency instruction
- vocabulary instruction
- text comprehension instruction

Like other studies before it, the NRP report shows how staff development in literacy is important in relation to children's literacy achievement. This study elaborates on how training teachers to use specific text comprehension strategies can impact children's overall improvement and reading comprehension achievement. It is through this early integration and comprehensive approach to balanced reading instruction that classroom teachers are able to combine the teaching of phonics, vocabulary, and specific reading comprehension strategies, resulting in the development of higher order thinking skills. First, young children learn how to read, and later, they read how to learn.

Limitations of the Study

Joanne Yatvin, the only elementary teacher member of the National Reading Panel, felt strongly enough to write a minority report to express a view that she believed was not considered by the more scholarly, science-based researchers of the Panel (NICHD, 2000, pp. 1–3). Some of Yatvin's concerns, which follow, might likely be supported by many classroom teachers, reading teachers, and parents:

- The Panel's reviews do not touch on early learning and home-support for literacy—matters which many experts believe are the critical determinants of school success or failure.
- The research on language development, emergent reading, understanding conventions of print, and all the other experiences that prepare young children to learn also demanded the Panel's attention. What the Panel did not consider in most cases were the school and classroom realities that make some types of instruction difficult—even impossible—to implement.

Yatvin's most critical complaint, however, is that she does not believe that the Panel fully responded to Congress's original charge. She writes that the report does not answer the most central question: What is known about the basic process by which children learn to read? (p. 3). In her view, Yatvin cites the seven questions that the National Institute of Child Health and Human Development (NICHD)—which had convened the Panel—had ignored.

- What is known about the basic processes by which children learn to read?
- What are the most common instructional approaches to teach children to read?
- What assessments have been made of the effectiveness of each of these methodologies in teaching critical reading skills?
- What does the Panel conclude about the readiness for implementation in the classroom of these research results?
- What do studies show about the effectiveness of teacher training in reading, and how can this knowledge be applied to improve this training?
- What practical findings from the Panel's report can be used by parents, teachers, and others to help teach children how to read?
- What important gaps remain in our knowledge of how children learn to read?

Yatvin states that the Panel does not adequately answer these key questions and that it had decided arbitrarily to respond only to the main areas outlined at the outset of the report. Yatvin also concedes that Congress had given the Panel an unrealistic timeframe in which to accomplish all of its demands. Finally, Yatvin states that she believes that to provide a balanced response to the Panel's research findings and conclusions, teacher reviewers should have been brought in to critique the Panel's conclusions before being released to the public.

The NRP report is based ultimately on scientifically based research and, as stated previously, lacks the balance of a qualitative perspective. I also believe that a more balanced approach to research is essential as well; more qualitative research—action research, formative evaluation, and participant observation designs—are necessary if research is going to truly serve practitioners' needs. It is obvious that the dearth of recommendations surrounding important areas such as technology and computer instruction, teaching reading to English language learners, and investigations into ameliorating disparity for nonwhite students requires more than quantitative studies such as scientific, control group, and laboratory studies, which simulate real literacy and balanced reading programs. In response to the need to address English language learners, the Panel explains that it did not address this vital literacy area because a new, comprehensive study was forthcoming from the Office of Educational Research and Improvement and NICHD. However, to date, this study has not appeared. Also, very much absent from the NRP report are recommendations for dealing with the disparity problems still plaguing African American and Latino children.

James Cunningham (2001) also raises a number of issues related to the efficacy of the so-called "scientific, experimental and quasi-experimental research" (p. 331) of the NRP, conducted by each of the five subgroups. In essence, Cunningham (2001) argues that the Panel's philosophy of science and doctrine of research design are seriously flawed, and then poses the rhetorical question "does that mean its findings are inevitably also flawed?" (p. 331). Cunningham proceeds by analyzing the actual findings and determinations of the five subgroups in question. With regard to phonemic awareness, Cunningham argues that the NRP ignores such literacy issues as "What are the long-term effects on silent reading comprehension ability, the reading habit, and attitudes toward reading, self, and school of its recommended changes in early reading instruction?" (p. 331). He also argues that the Panel ignores discussing the quality of instruction provided within the control groups, which could contribute to improvements that might not be totally contributable to a given methodology (phonemic awareness in this case). Cunningham (2001) also raises methodological issues with regard to the Panel's mixing of oral, silent, and independent fluency reading treatments, while concluding that on a short-term basis, "guided oral reading, especially repeated reading, leads to improved oral reading fluency" (p. 333). Perhaps the most important issue raised by Cunningham (also addressed by Roller, 2000), is that the formation of the NRP might be "a bold attempt by powerful political forces to gain control of reading research?" (p. 335). Cunningham answers his own question by stating "That will depend on whether persuasion or enforcement was the goal, and only time will tell" (p. 335).

Cunningham's rhetorical question about "powerful political forces" attempting to gain control of future reading research continues to be a serious issue. The National Council of Teachers of English (NCTE) states that the Reading First initiative is the culmination of a recent trend, as the federal government has increasingly attempted to define what reading is, to limit what counts as research on reading, and to dictate how reading should be taught in our classrooms. As a consequence, the government is channeling education funding to a few corporate purveyors of a limited set of methods of reading instruction. (2002, p. 1)

The Reading First initiative of the No Child Left Behind Act of 2001 states that a major goal is the implementation of scientifically based reading programs and practices in K–3 classrooms in order to assist all students to read on grade level by the end of grade 3. It is noteworthy that this is the first major federally sponsored reading grant to be issued since the NRP report in 2000. Cunningham's (2001) concerns that the formation of the National Reading Panel may have been, in part, to enforce the use of scientifically based research on future literacy funding opportunities seem to have been prophetic after all. For instance, Robert E. Slavin (2003) writes that the "key issue in the recent No Child Left Behind legislation is the distinction beween programs that are based on scientifically based research and those that have been evaluated in valid scientific experiments" (p. 15). Scientifically based research is defined here as "rigorous systematic, and objective procedures to obtain valid knowledge" (p. 12).

Two years after the NRP report was published, the Reading First initiative made $900 million available to states across the nation for improving reading. However, these funds, according to NCTE (2002), are "based upon and limited to the view of reading instruction embodied in the Reading First Initiative" (p. 1), which stems from its dependence on the NRP report as its research base. NCTE addresses the concern that the NRP "does not represent the full range of scientifically valid research methodology, but appears to have been chosen as selective support for a preconceived notion of what constitutes best practice" (p. 1).

Naturally, I am concerned about how involved the U.S. government is with regard to defining what reading is and what research methodology should be. I am encouraged, however, to see that two of the largest literacy-based associations—the International Reading Association and National Council of Teachers of English—are faithful "watch-dogs" of this recent political and legislative involvement in literacy policies.

In conclusion, on one hand, the reading wars seem to have abated with regard to finding a common ground for a more balanced approach to beginning reading instruction. On the other hand, my greatest concern is how can we seek a balanced approach to reading instruction if we do not seek a balanced approach to reading research?

SUMMARY

From a historical perspective, much has changed in the reading field during the past three decades since Chall's (1967) *Learning to Read: The Great Debate* was written. In 1967, only four years before the 1971 National Assessment of Educational Programs (NAEP) first began measuring the reading achievement of young children and adolescents, the reading scores of black, Hispanic, and white children were compared and reported for the first time. Although disparity in reading had not been as serious a concern at that time, the recognition that the problem existed was recorded publicly for the first time, and the United States became consciously aware that disparity was to be a new reality in literacy assessment as well as in the social consciousness. In 1997, Arletta Ingram Willis and Violet J. Harris wrote, "We would like to see more cooperative reading research efforts that include a plurality of voices and perspectives framed upon a commitment to social change and improvement" (p. 104). Indeed, this opportunity must be seized if we are ever to close this ever-widening racial gap in reading proficiency.

The times have caused dramatic changes for entry into the 21st century and for literacy in our new technological and global multicultural society. These changes caused by rapidly shifting demographics are affecting the lives of families, neighborhoods, and schools. New populations and greater numbers of low-socioeconomic minorities new to the English language continue to enter U.S. schools daily. As a result, teaching children how to read today has become dramatically more difficult than Chall or Bond and Dykstra could have possibly imagined in 1967.

Furthermore, *Preventing Reading Difficulties in Young Children* (Snow, Burns, & Griffin, 1998) and the National Reading Panel report (2000) have provided substantial evidence that Bond and Dykstra's First-Grade Studies (1967/1997) recommendations about the need for future research to focus on "teacher and learning situation characteristics rather than method and materials" (1997, p. 416) were indeed prophetic and will remain a lasting contribution to the field of literacy research.

A Balanced Approach to Beginning Reading Instruction: A Synthesis of Six Major U.S. Research Studies provides a summary and analysis of each of these research studies conducted from 1967 to 2000. Conclusions drawn from these studies show that there is a great deal of consensus on several key components of literacy, which is believed to support a balanced approach to teaching reading. One thing is for sure: Phonics instruction must be a part of a balanced approach to reading. How much phonics should be taught or which approaches are superior are questions research still has not resolved completely. It is likely that research will never be able to fully answer these overwhelming questions. Perhaps, as Dixie Lee Spiegel, former chair of the Balanced Reading Instruction Special Interest Group of the International Reading Association, states, that group's philosophy included "promoting instruction that avoids limiting teachers in their choices of methodologies and materials due to a singular reliance on any one program or set of instructional practices that claims to be the best approach for all learners" (Spiegel, as cited in Freppon & Dahl, 1998, p. 246). The research has taught us over and over again that there is no one best approach to reading. Chall (1967) certainly was emphatic in drawing this immutable conclusion more than 30 years ago.

Regardless, all the studies conclude that phonics must be taught systematically, not haphazardly or only in "teachable moments." On the other hand, all the studies (even Chall's to some extent) concur that phonics cannot be taught separately from reading meaningful text. Each of the studies addresses the importance of children's opportunities to read and write widely and independently in class and at home. Moderation and balance in instruction are supported in each of the studies, and balance is presented in various strengths along the continuum of instruction. P. David Pearson puts into perspective a kind of balance that seems to move disparate factions supporting either a skills approach or a whole language approach closer toward a common ground (Pearson, as cited in Freppon & Dahl, 1998):

> The first principle [for balanced instruction] is
> • Teachers build code-based instruction on their deep knowledge of language and learning.

- [Teachers] take advantage of the natural (though not identical) relationship between oral and written language and use it to help children learn from the language wellspring deep in their being.
- Once children discover the principle of representing their words with the letters they are learning, they are helped to embrace the alphabetic principle.
- [Children] acquire a concept for the whole system of representation.
- Good practice grounded in deep knowledge of language and literacy will lead [teachers] to regard learning to read as an intellectual achievement rather than an acquisition of skills. (p. 247)

What Pearson and all the researchers throughout this book have concluded is that learning the letters and sounds of language is necessary, but teachers need to apply this principle with common sense. Excessive drill is not necessary. Good sensible teaching, however, is required in teaching the letters and sounds of language whether it is in using a whole-part-whole approach, an onset-rime approach, or a more synthetic phonics approach. We must remember that no one approach is better than another, and that phonics is a means to an end that can be taught while using the best children's literature to help beginning readers learn to read skillfully and fluently for meaning and enjoyment. This balanced approach is taught effectively in guided reading groups that scaffold reading experiences while engaging children in different phases of reading, including prereading, during-reading, and after-reading activities.

Reading comprehension is discussed throughout the six research studies culminating with the NRP report. Conclusions from several studies show that by developing vocabulary knowledge, reading fluency, specific comprehension reading strategies, while using multiple reading activities together with positive teacher feedback, children improve their overall reading comprehension. Although reading comprehension was discussed throughout each study reported in this book, researchers did not give as much attention to this important area as it relates to beginning reading instruction. Consequently, more research is required in the areas of reading comprehension, specific content areas, and critical reading. Although research in this area is being conducted by the RAND Reading Study Group, this study is investigating reading for understanding at the middle school and secondary level. However, it is my strong belief that further research is necessary in developing reading comprehension in young readers, and the RAND study should include this on its agenda.

Another area requiring a national research initiative is in the area of English language learner literacy acquisition. Upon reading these major, nationally sponsored literacy research studies, I find it inconceivable that the profession has such a lack of information related to teaching reading to English language learners—an ever increasing diverse population—who need to know how to read more and better than ever before in U.S. history.

According to the NRP report, this important issue was not investigated because it was to become a major study by the National Institute of Child Health and Human Development. Unfortunately, no report has been forthcoming at the time of this publication. Finally, a national initiative is necessary to combat reading disparity issues related to African American, Latino, and Native American populations. It is evident that a gap continues to widen to the detriment of these and other people of color in the United States. As we have seen throughout this book, literacy issues are far too complex to look for easy solutions, but as Willis and Harris (1997) have observed, a national initiative has not yet been convened to investigate reading issues necessary to resolve this national literacy problem.

I, however, am confident that these major initiatives will be realized. Some are beginning and some are within our grasp; others may soon appear or are on the horizon. Fortunately, we have completed research on more than 30 years of beginning reading instruction to help settle the reading wars. Soon, we can really begin teaching young children to read more successfully than ever before. Once we have gone beyond the rhetoric and have left no child behind, we may breathe a sigh of relief that we have met the greatest educational challenge of this millennium's first decade: that each of our youngest learners will learn to read.

Activities for Applying Literacy Concepts

1. Review one or more new basal reading series published within the last five years. Based on your reading of *A Balanced Approach to Beginning Reading Instruction: A Synthesis of Six Major U.S. Research Studies*, check to see how effectively you believe each basal (a) is organized, (b) introduces phonics, (c) integrates phonics with meaningful text, (d) uses authentic stories, (e) presents specific comprehension strategies, and (f) develops vocabulary.

2. Observe a classroom teacher who teaches reading without a basal reader. Determine if he or she uses a balanced reading approach. How does he or she teach phonics? Are children learning how to decode words effectively in his or her classroom? Is authentic reading of books used effectively? How are the children's comprehension skills taught? Do children in the class find reading fun? Keep an ongoing account of your findings in a journal.

3. Below is an analogy or extended metaphor that explains the process of reading. Anderson, Hiebert, Scott, and Wilkinson (1985) compare how reading is analogous to the performance of a symphony orchestra. First, read the analogy. Then, with one or more members from your cooperative group, try to create your own analogy or metaphor related to the reading process.

Reading can be compared to the performance of a symphony orchestra. This analogy illustrates three points. First, like the performance of a symphony, reading is a holistic act. In other words, while reading can be analyzed into subskills such as discriminating letters and identifying words, performing the subskills one at a time does not constitute reading. Reading can be said to take place only when the parts are put together in a smooth, integrated performance. Second, success in reading comes from practice over long periods of time, like skill in playing musical instruments. Indeed, it is a lifelong endeavor. Third, as with a musical score, there may be more than one interpretation of a text. The interpretation depends upon the background of the reader, the purpose for reading, and the context in which reading occurs.

(From Anderson et al. (1985). *Becoming a Nation of Readers: The Report of the Commission on Reading*, p. 7.)

4. Share your group's analogy on the reading process. Then listen to the other groups present their analogies. Discuss how they are similar, yet unique. Assess these examples for their aesthetic (creative) and efferent (cognitive) qualities. How do they compare to the model provided?

5. Similar to the analogy discussed in number 3, Adams (1990a, p. 3; 1990b, p. 19) has also created her own analogy, comparing the operation of the reading system to the engine of a car from *Beginning to Read: Thinking and Learning About Print.* Read Adams's analogy and compare it to that of Anderson et al. Of the two, which one do you like best? Explain why.

To clarify the relation of word recognition processes to the rest of the system, an analogy might be useful. Let's say that the system that supports our ability to read is like a car. Within this analogy, print is like gas. The engine and the mechanics of the car are the perceptual and conceptual machinery that make the car go.

It is obvious that print is essential to reading—no gas, no driving. But print alone is not enough to make the reading system go. Just as cars will not start without spark plugs, reading cannot begin without the spark of recognition. And while cars require more than one spark plug for power and smoothness of operation, so the reading system processes more than one letter at once and in coordination. Associations among letters, like the crankshaft in a car, keep the reading system rolling—despite occasional problems. The letter that is misperceived or even illegible does not stop the reading machine, any more than the occasional misfire of a spark plug will stop a car.

But the engine is only indirectly responsible for making a car go. The engine turns gas to kinetic energy, and the energy turns the wheels. Similarly, the perceptual system turns print to mental energy, such that it can be understood.

Obviously a car *couldn't* be driven without gas, without spark plugs, without a crankshaft, and without a differential and wheels.

But it is also important to recognize that it *wouldn't* be driven if it didn't run well. Imagine that you had to push a button every time you wanted a spark plug to fire. Imagine that the car would only go a couple of miles per hour or that it unpredictably stalled every few moments. You would very likely choose not to drive at all.

By the same token, readers who are unable to recognize individual letters and spelling patterns quickly, effortlessly, and automatically and to transform them to words and meanings are very likely to choose not to read at all. To the extent that children do not read, they do not get the practice with letters and letter patterns needed to make efficient their perception. And so they continue to have difficulty reading, falling farther and farther behind their peers as they get older.

Clearly, without gas and without an engine and mechanics in adequate working order, a car won't go. Suppose, however, that your reading system has plenty of print to consume and a fine mechanical system. Are you on your way?

No. First, you have to want to go somewhere, and you have to have some idea of how to get there. As you travel, you must monitor and control your route, periodically take assessment of how far you've gone, and make sure you're on the right road. You must also pay careful attention to the details of the road and control your car through them. Depending on such variables as the familiarity of the route and whether it is bumpy, windy, congested, or unpredictable, you will have to invest considerable active attention in your progress.

Similarly, understanding texts that are unfamiliar in concept or difficult in wording requires your active attention. But the more you direct attention to the *mechanics* of reading, the less attention you have available to support *understanding*. Only if your ability to recognize and capture the meanings of words is rapid, effortless, and automatic will you have available the cognitive energy and resources upon which comprehension depends.

As it happens, *everybody* wants to go someplace. Everybody wants stimulation and the sense of growth and accomplishment that comes with meeting challenges. If reading is unstimulating or unproductive, some individuals will choose other ways to spend their time. If reading seems aversive, some will avoid it altogether. Forty percent of the fourth-grade poor readers in a Texas school recently claimed that they would rather clean their rooms than read. One child stated, "I'd rather clean the mold around the bathtub than read."

Fortunately, for purposes of schooling, most young children go almost anywhere they are led—so long as they are not frustrated, unsuccessful, or bored. But even as this eases our task as reading educators, it greatly increases our responsibility. It is up to us to lead our children in the right direction.

And it is here that the car analogy breaks down. So apt for describing the operation of the system, it is wholly inappropriate for modeling its acquisition. Building a car is a modular, hierarchical activity. From the bottom up, the discrete parts of the car's subsystems are fastened together. Then, one by one, the subsystems are connected to each other.

In contrast, the parts of the reading system are not discrete. We cannot proceed by completing each individual subsystem and then fastening it to another. Rather, the parts of the reading system must *grow* together. They must grow to one another and from one another.

For the connections and even the connected parts to develop properly, they must be linked in the very course of acquisition. And this dependency works in both directions. We cannot properly develop the higher order processes without due attention to the lower; we cannot focus on the lower order processes without constantly clarifying and exercising their connections to the higher.

It is only when we understand the parts of the system and their interrelations that we can reflect methodically and productively on the needs and progress of each of our students.

(From Adams, M.J. (1990), *Beginning to Read: Thinking and Learning about Print: A Summary* [pp. 19–21]. Copyright 1990 Massachusetts Institute of Technology. Reprinted with permission.)

6. Write a unit plan that includes several lesson plans, demonstrating how a teacher of beginning reading can teach effectively and creatively in an integrated and comprehensive balanced reading program. Develop at least two weeks of lesson plans for a specific grade level, demonstrating how children can learn to love reading while learning to develop the necessary supportive skills that will make them successful lifelong readers.

Questions for Cooperative Discussion Groups

1. Discuss the questions raised in the opening paragraph of the Preface of this book. How many of these difficult questions can you now answer fully? Are there questions that you still cannot answer? If so, do these unanswered questions require more research on your part? Consider how you might research any remaining difficult questions about reading. Are there questions that might never be answered with certainty?

2. Raise and discuss other questions that you have about any of the research findings you have read. Are you confused about any of the researchers' conclusions? Do you disagree with any of the findings or conclusions?

3. In lieu of so much discussion about phonics, fluency, and comprehension skills, discuss how an exemplary teacher can motivate young children to read for the love of reading so they become lifelong readers. Compare your list with a peer.

4. At the end of chapters 2 through 7, two sections appear: Strengths of the Study and Limitations of the Study. Discuss these two sections at the end of each of the six studies and add your readers' perspectives by extending the strengths and/or weaknesses in each.

5. Compare and contrast your cooperative group's perspectives related to the strengths and weaknesses in selected research studies.

REFERENCES

Adams, M.J. (1990a). *Beginning to read: Thinking and learning about print.* Cambridge, MA: MIT Press.

Adams, M.J. (1990b). *Beginning to read: Thinking and learning about print: A summary* (Prepared by S.A. Stahl, J. Osborn, & F. Lehr). Urbana, IL: University of Illinois, Center for the Study of Reading.

Adams, M.J. (1998). The three-cueing system. In J. Osborn & F. Lehr (Eds.), *Literacy for all: Issues in teaching and learning* (pp. 73–99). New York: Guilford.

Alexander, P.A., & Jetton, T.L. (2000). Learning from text: A multidimensional and developmental perspective. In M.L. Kamil, P.B. Mosenthal, P.D. Pearson, & R. Barr (Eds.), *Handbook of reading research* (Vol. 3, pp. 563–586). Mahwah, NJ: Erlbaum.

Anderson, R.C., Hiebert, E.H., Scott, J.A., & Wilkinson, I.A.G. (1985). *Becoming a nation of readers: The report of the Commission on Reading.* Washington, DC: National Institute of Education.

Armbruster, B.B., Lehr, F., & Osborn, J. (2001). *Put reading first: The research building blocks for teaching children to read.* Washington, DC: U.S. Department of Education.

Bear, D.R., Invernizzi, M., Templeton, S., & Johnston, F. (2000). *Words their way: Word study for phonics, vocabulary, and spelling instruction.* Upper Saddle River, NJ: Prentice-Hall.

Biddle, B.J., & Berliner, D.C. (2002). A research synthesis: Small class size and its effects. *Education Leadership, 59,* 12–23.

Block, C.C., & Mangieri, J.N. (2002). Recreational reading: 20 years later. *The Reading Teacher, 55,* 572–585.

Bloom, B.S. (1956). *Taxonomy of educational objectives: Part I, Cognitive Domain.* New York: Longmans Green.

Bond, G.I., & Dykstra, R. (1967). The cooperative research program in first-grade reading instruction. *Reading Research Quarterly, 2,* 5–142.

Bond, G.I., & Dykstra, R. (1997). The cooperative research program in first-grade reading instruction. *Reading Research Quarterly, 32,* 345–427.

Bowler, R. (2000, September 3). Racial, ethnic disparities in national reading scores remain troubling, constant [The Education Beat]. *The Sun* [Baltimore], p. B2.

Calkins, L.M. (1986). *The art of teaching writing.* Portsmouth, NH: Heinemann.

Cassidy, J., & Wenrich, J.K. (1998, February/March). What's hot, what's not for 1998. *Reading Today, 15*(4), pp. 1, 28.

Chall, J.S. (1967). *Learning to read: The great debate.* New York: McGraw Hill.

Chall, J.S. (1980). Should we teach the basics or the humanities in reading? Humanism and the basics. *The Reading Instruction Journal, 3,* 57–58.

Chall, J.S. (1985). Afterword. In R.C. Anderson et al., *Becoming a nation of readers: The report on the Commission on Reading* (pp. 123–125). Washington, DC: National Institute of Education.

Chall, J.S. (1999). Commentary: Some thoughts on reading research. *Reading Research Quarterly, 34,* 8–10.

Clay, M.M. (1991). *Becoming literate: The construction of inner control.* Portsmouth, NH: Heinemann.

Clay, M.M. (1993). *Reading Recovery: A guidebook for teachers in training.* Portsmouth, NH: Heinemann.

Cowen, J.E. (1983). Reading teacher as evaluator: An emerging role. *The Reading Instruction Journal, 1,* 3–7.

Cowen, J.E. (1999/2000). Using Louise M. Rosenblatt's "aesthetic stance" to teach children how to read a poem. *The Reading Instruction Journal, 45,* 4–7.

Cowen, J.E. (2001). An action research model for changing teaching behaviors and literacy achievement for young children. *Journal of the New Jersey Association of Teacher Educators, 10,* 51–60.

Cowen, J.E. (in press). Essential elements of a balanced literacy program. *The Reading Instruction Journal.*

Cunningham, J.W. (2001). Essay book review. *The National Reading Panel Report. Reading Research Quarterly, 36,* 326–335.

Cunningham, P.M. (2000). *Phonics they use: Words for reading and writing* (3rd ed.). New York: Longman.

Ehri, L.C., Nunes, S.R., Willows, D.M., Schuster, B.V., Yaghoub-Zadeh, Z., & Shanahan, T. (2001). Phonemic awareness instruction helps children learn to read: Evidence from the National Reading Panel's meta-analysis. *Reading Research Quarterly, 36,* 250–287.

Elbow, P. (1981). *Writing with power: Techniques for mastering the writing process.* New York: Oxford University Press.

Flesch, R. (1955). *Why Johnny can't read.* New York: Harper.

Fletcher, R. (1993). *What a writer needs.* Portsmouth, NH: Heinemann.

Fountas, I.C., & Pinnell, G.S. (1996). *Guided reading: Good first teaching for all children.* Portsmouth, NH: Heinemann.

Freppon, P.A., & Dahl, K.L. (1998). Balanced instruction: Insights and considerations. *Reading Research Quarterly, 33,* 240–251.

Gaffney, J.S., & Anderson, R.C. (2000). Trends in reading research in the United States: Changing intellectual currents over three decades. In M.L. Kamil, P.B. Mosenthall, P.D. Pearson, & R. Barr (Eds.), *Handbook of reading research* (Vol. 3, pp. 53–74). Mahwah, NJ: Erlbaum.

Graves, D. (1983). *Writing: Teachers and children at work.* Portsmouth, NH: Heinemann.

Graves, M.F., & Dykstra, R. (1997). Contextualizing the First-Grade Studies: What is the best way to teach children to read? *Reading Research Quarterly, 32,* 342–344.

Harste, J. (1999). *Balanced reading instruction: Part of the problem or part of the solution*. Presentation at the Annual Convention of the International Reading Association, San Diego, CA.

Holdaway, D. (1979). *The foundations of literacy*. Sydney: Ashton Scholastic.

Johnson, D. (1999). *Balanced reading instruction: Review of literature*. Retrieved November 15, 2002, from http://www.ncrel.org/sdrs/timely/bripub.htm

Joyce, B., & Showers, B. (1988). *Student achievement through staff development*. New York: Longman.

Moats, L.C. (2000). *Whole language lives on: The illusion of "balanced" reading instruction*. Retrieved January 8, 2003, from http://www.edexcellence.net/library/wholelang/moats.html

Morrow, L.M., Tracey, D.H., Woo, D.G., & Pressley, M. (1999). Characteristics of exemplary first-grade literacy instruction. *The Reading Teacher, 52*, 462–476.

Murray, D.M. (1968). *A writer teaches writing*. Boston: Houghton Mifflin.

National Commission on Excellence in Education (NCEE). (1983). *A nation at risk: The imperative for educational reform*. Washington, DC: U.S. Department of Education.

National Council of Teachers of English (NCTE). (2002). *Resolutions: On the Reading First Initiative*. NCTE annual business meeting, Atlanta, GA. Retrieved January 29, 2003, from http://www.ncte.org/resolutions/readingfirst2002.shtml

National Institute of Child Health and Human Development (NICHD). (2000). *Report of the National Reading Panel: Teaching children to read: An evidence-based assessment of the scientific research literature on reading and its implications for reading instruction* (NIH Publication No. 00-4769). Washington, DC: U.S. Government Printing Office.

Pearson, P.D. (1997). The First-Grade Studies: A personal reflection. *Reading Research Quarterly, 32*, 428–432.

Pearson, P.D. (1999). A historically based review of *Preventing Reading Difficulties in Young Children. Reading Research Quarterly, 2*, 231–246.

Pearson, P.D. (2001). Foreword. In M.J. Adams, *Beginning to read: Thinking and learning about print* (p. v, 14th printing). Cambridge, MA: MIT Press.

Phoenix, P. (1964). *Realms of meaning*. New York: McGraw-Hill.

Pinnell, G.S., & Fountas, I.C. (1998). *Word matters: Teaching phonics and spelling in the reading/writing classroom*. Portsmouth, NH: Heinemann.

Pressley, M. (2000). What should comprehension instruction be the instruction of? In M.L. Kamil, P.B. Mosenthal, P.D. Pearson, & R. Barr (Eds.), *Handbook of reading research* (Vol. 3, pp. 545–556). Mahwah, NJ: Erlbaum.

Pressley, M. (2002). *Reading instruction that works: The case for balanced teaching* (2nd ed.). New York: Guilford.

Pressley, M., Wharton-McDonald, R., Hampston, J.M., & Echevarria, M. (1998). The nature of literacy instruction in ten grade 4 and 5 classrooms in upstate New York. *Scientific Studies of Reading, 2*, 159–191.

RAND Reading Study Group. (2002). *Reading for understanding: Toward an R & D program in reading comprehension*. Santa Monica, CA: Author.

Reutzel, D.R. (1999). On balanced reading. *The Reading Teacher, 52,* 322–324.

Richgels, D.J. (2001). Phonemic awareness. *The Reading Teacher, 55,* 274–278.

Roller, C. (2000). The International Reading Association responds to a highly charged policy environment. *The Reading Teacher, 53,* 626–636.

Rothstein, R. (2001, September 5). Lessons: Consensus in reading war: If sides would only look [Metro Education]. *The New York Times,* p. B7.

Routman, R. (1988). *Transitions: From literature to literacy.* Portsmouth, NH: Heinemann.

Routman, R. (1994). *Invitations: Changes in teachers and learners, K–12.* Portsmouth, NH: Heinemann.

Searfoss, L.W. (1997). Connecting the past with the present: The legacy and spirit of the First-Grade Studies. *Reading Research Quarterly, 32,* 433–438.

Seidenberg, M. (1990). Order form for the book. *Beginning to read: Thinking and learning about print: A summary* (Prepared by S.A. Stahl, J. Osborn, & F. Lehr). Urbana, IL: University of Illinois, Center for the Study of Reading.

Shaefer, R.J. (1967). *The school as a center of inquiry.* New York: Harper and Row.

Slavin, R.E. (2003). A reader's guide to scientifically based research. *Educational Leadership, 60,* 12–16.

Smith, F. (1984). *Reading without nonsense.* New York: Teachers College Press.

Snow, C.E., Burns, S., & Griffin, P. (Eds.). (1998). *Preventing reading difficulties in young children.* Washington, DC: National Academy Press.

Spiegel, D.L. (1998). Silver bullets, babies, and bath water: Literature response groups in a balanced literacy program. *The Reading Teacher, 52,* 114–124.

Stebbins, L.B., St. Pierre, R.G., Proper, E.C., Anderson, R.B., & Cerva, T.R. (1977). *Education as experimentation: A planned variation model* (Vol. 4-A) An evaluation of Project Follow Through. Cambridge, MA: ABT Associates.

Strickland, D.S. (1998). *Teaching phonics today: A primer for educators.* Newark, DE: International Reading Association.

Strickland, D.S., & Cullinan, B. (1990). Afterword. In M.J. Adams, *Beginning to read: Thinking and learning about print* (pp. 425–434). Cambridge, MA: MIT Press.

Tompkins, G.E. (1997). *Literacy for the 21st Century: A balanced approach.* Upper Saddle River, NJ: Merrill, Prentice Hall.

Vail, P.L. (1991). *Common ground: Whole language and phonics working together.* Rosemont, NJ: Modern Learning Press.

Vygotsky, L.S. (1978). *Mind in society: The development of higher psychological processes* (M. Cole, V. John-Steiner, S. Scribner, & E. Souberman, Eds. and Trans.). Cambridge, MA: Harvard University Press. (Original work published 1934)

Weaver, C. (Ed.). (1998). *Reconsidering a balanced approach to reading.* Urbana, IL: National Council of Teachers of English.

Wharton-McDonald, R., Pressley, M., Rankin, J., Mistretta, J., Yokoi, L., & Ettenberger, S. (1997). Effective primary-grades literacy instruction = balanced literacy instruction. *The Reading Teacher, 50,* 518–521.

Willis, I.W., & Harris, V.J. (1997). Expanding the boundaries: A reaction to the First-Grade Studies. *Reading Research Quarterly, 32,* 439–445.

INDEX

Note: Page numbers followed by *f* indicate figures; those followed by *t* indicate tables.

A

A Nation at Risk (National Commission on Excellence in Education), 30, 36

ACHIEVEMENT: and alphabet instruction, 16–18, 19, 41; and basal readers, 16–18; and class size, 15; and emergent literacy, 18–19; and integrated approach, 17; and letter recognition, 9, 41; and linguistic approach, 16–18; of minority students, 37; of non-English speakers, 37; and phonemic awareness, 19, 41, 43–44; and phonics instruction, 16–18; predictors of, 41; and staff development, 14–15; and student characteristics, 13; and teacher characteristics, 13; and teacher education, 14–15

ACTION RESEARCH MODEL, 14

ACTIVITIES, TEACHER, 83–86

ADAMS, M.J., 1, 3, 6, 19, 21, 27, 28, 29, 31, 34, 35, 37, 39–51, 66, 72, 84

ALEXANDER, P.A., 5

ALPHABET INSTRUCTION: and achievement, 16–18, 19, 41; importance of, 19

AMBUSHER, F.F., 31

ANDERSON, R.B., 50, 60, 66, 83

ANDERSON, R.C., 1, 30–39, 41

ARMBRUSTER, B.B., 72

ASSESSMENT, FLUENCY, 68. *See also* observation

ASSOCIATION METHODS, 69

AUTHENTICITY, 56

AUTOMATIC PROCESSING, 43

B

BALANCED READING APPROACH: bias in literature about, 3–4; buying programs for, 7; characteristics of, 4; complexity of, 2; components of, 4, 5–6; definition of, 10, 54; effects of a lack of definition of, 7; essential elements of, 8–9; moderation in, 5; in

New Zealand, 5–6; peak of, 40; principles of, 80–81; teachers' support for, 1; and technology, 48; using research to find, 2

BASAL READERS: and achievement, 16–18; alignment of research with, 25–26; components of, 17; controlled vocabulary in, 33; versus integrated approach, 17; phonics instruction in, 17, 29; recommended, 32–33

BEAR, D.R., 28

BECOMING A NATION OF READERS: THE REPORT OF THE COMMISSION ON READING (ANDERSON, HIEBERT, SCOTT, & WILKINSON): history of, 30–31; limitations of study in, 37–38; results of study in, 32–36; strengths of study in, 36

BEGINNING TO READ: THINKING AND LEARNING ABOUT PRINT (ADAMS), 1, 29; history of, 39; limitations of study in, 49–51; results of study in, 40–47; strengths of study in, 47–49

BERLINER, D.C., 15

BIAS, 3–4

BIDDLE, B.J., 15

BLOCK, C.C., 67

BLOOM, B.S., 23

BNR. *See Becoming a Nation of Readers: The Report of the Commission on Reading*

BOND, G.I., 11–13, 15, 17–22, 24, 28, 36, 37, 41, 50

BOWLER, R., 58

BURNS, S., 5, 14, 17, 18, 21, 23, 27, 52–60, 61

BUSH, G.W., 62

C

CALIFORNIA EDUCATIONAL SYSTEM, 40

CAPACITY METHODS, 69

CASSIDY, J., 8

CENTER FOR THE STUDY OF READING, 30

CERVA, T.R., 50

CHALL, J.S., 3, 11–12, 17, 18, 21, 22–29, 31, 36, 37, 39, 41, 50, 51, 59, 60, 79, 80

CHILDREN. *See students*

CLASS SIZE, 15

CLAY, M.C., 1, 6, 19, 20, 41, 48

COACHING, 14–15

CODE INSTRUCTION. *See* phonics instruction

COLD WAR, 11

COMMUNITY: characteristics of, 15–16; and reading preparedness, 45–46

CONTEXT PROCESS, 47*f*

CONTROLLED VOCABULARY: versus new basal readers, 33; usefulness of, 20

COOPERATIVE RESEARCH PROGRAM IN FIRST-GRADE READING INSTRUCTION (BOND & DYKSTRA), 11

COWEN, J.E., 7, 8, 14, 31, 41, 67

CUEING SYSTEMS, 6–7

CULLINAN, B., 49–50, 59

CUNNINGHAM, J.W., 76–77

CUNNINGHAM, P.M., 1

CURRICULUM, READING, 54–55

CURRICULUM REFORM MOVEMENT, 22–23

D

DAHL, K.L., 3, 6, 7, 80

DEAR. *See* DROP EVERYTHING AND READ

DEMONSTRATION, 14–15

DIRECT INSTRUCTION: amount of time spent on, 34; need for, 43; through literature, 25. *See also* explicit instruction

DISCUSSION GROUPS, 67, 87

DRILL, 81

DROP EVERYTHING AND READ (DEAR), 67

DYKSTRA, R., 11–12, 13, 15, 17–22, 24, 28, 36, 37, 41, 50

E

ECONOMY, 30

EHRI, L.C., 42

EMERGENT LITERACY, 18–19

ETTENBERGER, S., 7

EXPLICIT INSTRUCTION, 69. *See also* direct instruction

F

FAIRY TALES, 26

FIRST GRADE, 66

FIRST-GRADE STUDIES: and basal readers, 16–18; versus Chall's study, 24; and class size, 15–16; and community characteristics, 15–16; comparisons of literacy approaches in, 16–18; and emergent literacy, 18–19; history of, 11–12; limitations of, 21; overview of, 11; and phonics instruction, 16–18; research questions of, 12–19; and school characteristics, 15–16; strengths of, 19–21; and student characteristics, 13; and teacher characteristics, 13

FLESCH, R., 11, 22

FLUENCY: assessment of, 68; definition of, 67; extensive reading for, 24–25; and improved reading comprehension, 67; lack of, 68; relationship to reading comprehension, 73; techniques for improving, 67–68

FOLKTALES, 26

FOUNDATIONS IN LEARNING (TECHNOLOGY-BASED PROGRAM), 72

FOUNTAS, I., 1, 6

FREPPON, P.A., 3, 6, 7, 80

G

GAFFNEY, J.S., 1

GOODLING, W., 61

GORE, A., 62

GRAVES, D., 33

GRAVES, M.F., 11, 12

GRIFFIN, P., 5, 14, 17, 18, 21, 23, 27, 52–60, 61

GUIDED READING, 5

GUIDED REPEATED ORAL READING, 68

H

HARRIS, V.J., 12, 79, 82

HARSTE, J., 7

HIEBERT, E.H., 30–39, 41, 60, 66, 83

HIGHER ORDER THINKING SKILLS, 23, 73

HILLMAN, A.W., 14

HOLDAWAY, D., 5

HOME ENVIRONMENT, 45–46

HONIG, B., 40

"HOW SCHOOLS FAIL OUR CHILDREN" (AMBUSHER), 31

I

IMPLICIT INSTRUCTION, 69

INDEPENDENT READING: and improved reading comprehension, 67; and motivation, 43; time spent on, 34

INDIVIDUALIZED READING PROCEDURES, 5

INTEGRATED READING APPROACH, 5, 17, 34, 66

INTERNATIONAL READING ASSOCIATION (IRA), 62, 77

INTERVENTION PROGRAMS, 48, 50, 57

INVENTED SPELLING, 45, 49, 55

J–K

JEFFORDS, J., 62

JETTON, T.L., 5

JOHNSON, D., 6

JOHNSON, L.B., 12

JOYCE, B., 14

KINDERGARTEN: goals of, 56; phonemic awareness in, 27; phonics instruction in, 66; screening in, 57; writing in, 35

L

LANGUAGE EXPERIENCE APPROACH, 5, 16–18

LEARNING TO READ: THE GREAT DEBATE (CHALL), 21, 22–29, 39

LEHR, F., 39, 72

LETTER RECOGNITION, 19, 41

LINGUISTIC APPROACH, 16–18

LITERATURE: direct instruction through, 25; minority people in, 26; need for, 33; for phonics instruction, 25, 41, 44; providing opportunities to read, 32; for vocabulary practice, 43

LITERATURE CIRCLES, 67

LITTLE PLANET LITERACY SERIES (TECHNOLOGY-BASED PROGRAM), 72

LONG VOWELS, 45

LYON, G.R., 4–5

M

MANGIERI, J.N., 67

MEANING PROCESS, 47f

MISTSRETTA, J., 7

MOATS, L.C., 3, 4

MORROW, L.M., 36

MOTIVATION, STUDENT: importance of, 32; and independent reading, 43; and phonics instruction, 29; and transactional groups, 67

MULTIMEDIA, 69

N

NATIONAL ACADEMY OF EDUCATION, 30, 31

NATIONAL ACADEMY OF SCIENCES, 52

NATIONAL ASSESSMENT OF EDUCATIONAL PROGRESS (NAEP), 37, 40, 58, 79

NATIONAL COMMISSION ON EXCELLENCE IN EDUCATION (NCEE), 30

NATIONAL COUNCIL OF TEACHERS OF ENGLISH (NCTE), 62, 77

NATIONAL DEFENSE EDUCATION ACT, 11

NATIONAL INSTITUTE OF CHILD HEALTH AND HUMAN DEVELOPMENT (NICHD), 1, 14, 16, 24, 27, 28, 31, 61–78, 82

NATIONAL INSTITUTE OF EDUCATION, 30

NATIONAL INSTITUTES OF HEALTH (NIH), 4–5

NATIONAL READING PANEL, 14, 16, 24, 28, 31, 61–78. *See also Report of the National Reading Panel: Teaching Children to Read*

NCEE. *See* National Commission on Excellence in Education

NCTE. *See* National Council of Teachers of English

NEUMAN, S.B., 2

THE NEW FUN WITH DICK AND JANE SERIES, 33

NEW YORK TIMES MAGAZINE, 30–31

NEW YORK TIMES (NEWSPAPER), 4

NEW ZEALAND, 5–6, 41

NICHD. *See* National Institute of Child Health and Human Development

NIH. *See* National Institutes of Health

NO CHILD LEFT BEHIND ACT (2001), 77

NUNES, S.R., 42

O

OBSERVATION, 6–7, 29. *See also* assessment, fluency

OFFICE OF EDUCATIONAL RESEARCH AND IMPROVEMENT, 76

ONSET AND RIME APPROACH, 44–45, 66

ORTHOGRAPHIC PROCESS, 46, 47*f*

OSBORN, J., 39, 72

P–Q

PEARSON, P.D., 7, 21, 32, 49, 56, 58, 59, 60, 80

PHOENIX, P., 22

PHONEMIC AWARENESS: and achievement, 19, 41, 43–44; advantages of, 65; best instructional methods for, 42; definition of, 41, 73; importance of, 64; in kindergarten, 27; population for, 65; as prerequisite to phonics instruction, 41–42; software for, 65, 72

PHONICS, 73

PHONICS INSTRUCTION: and achievement, 16–18; advantages of, 18, 23–24; in basal readers, 17, 29; best methods of, 26, 32; in California educational system, 40; early introduction of, 65–66; effect on spelling skills, 28; in first grade, 66; goals of, 31–32, 49; and improved reading comprehension, 26; and invented spelling, 45, 49, 55; in kindergarten, 66; for low-income students, 24, 27; for low-performing students, 24, 66; for minority students, 26; as necessary component in reading instruction, 3; for older readers, 66; versus onset and rime approach, 44–45; as part of integrated approach, 66; phonemic awareness as prerequisite for, 41–42; scope-and-sequence approach to, 49; staff development in, 25; student motivation in, 29; teachers' view of, 1; time of, 31; in United Kingdom, 27; using literature for, 25, 41, 44; in whole language, 39

PHONOGRAMS, 44–45

PHONOLOGICAL PROCESS, 47*f*

PINNELL, G.S., 1, 6

POLITICS, 76–77

PRACTICE: need for, 43; in teacher education, 14–15; of vocabulary, 43

PRESSLEY, M., 2, 3–4, 7, 36

PREVENTING READING DIFFICULTIES IN YOUNG CHILDREN (SNOW, BURNS, & GRIFFIN), 23–24, 52–60, 61

PRINT CONCEPTS, 43

PROPER, E.C., 50

PSYCHOLOGY, 48, 59

PUNCTUATION, 67

PUT READING FIRST: THE RESEARCH BUILDING BLOCKS FOR TEACHING CHILDREN TO READ (ARMBRUSTER, LEHR, & OSBORN), 72

QUALITATIVE RESEARCH, 75

R

RAND READING STUDY GROUP, 81–82

RANKIN, J., 7

READING: curriculum for, 54–55; disparity in, 79; versus playing music, 35

READING ALOUD, 43, 46

READING COMPREHENSION: crucial areas of, 68–69; effect of vocabulary instruction on, 69; and effects of phonics instruction, 26; and fluency, 67; and independent reading, 67; relationship to vocabulary and fluency, 73; required skills for, 73–74; and text structure, 31

READING COMPREHENSION INSTRUCTION: Bloom's taxonomy in, 23; components of, 2–3

READING EXCELLENCE ACT (1997), 61–62

READING FIRST INITIATIVE, 77

READING INSTRUCTION: avoiding either-or thinking in, 5; challenges to, 79; curricula for, 54–55; goals of, 49, 54; learning from past, 7–8; phonics in, 3; principles of, 34–35; requirements of, 3, 53; spelling patterns in, 3; and teacher education, 70–71, 74; and technology, 71–72

READING INVENTORIES, 68

READING PROCESS, 46–47

READING PROFICIENCY, 53

READING READINESS: and home environment, 45–46; paradigm shift away from, 19

READING RECOVERY PROGRAM, 48, 50

READING STRATEGIES: need for, 33; teacher education in, 70

RECREATIONAL READING, 67

REFORM: of curriculum, 22–23; in the 1980s, 30–31

REPEATED READING, 68

REPORT OF THE NATIONAL READING PANEL: TEACHING CHILDREN TO READ (NATIONAL INSTITUTE OF CHILD HEALTH AND HUMAN DEVELOPMENT): findings of, 64–72; history of, 61–63; limitations of, 74–78; organization of, 64; research questions of, 63–64, 74–75; strengths of, 72–74; topics of study in, 63; website for, 64. See also National Reading Panel

RESEARCH: alignment of basal readers with, 25–26; design issues of, 60; distortion of, 3; exploration by teachers of, 2; improving methodologies for, 36; on minority students, 82; needed areas of, 81–82; on non–English speakers, 50–51, 82; and politics, 76–77; in technology, 71–72. *See also specific studies*

RESEARCHERS: teachers as, 14–15

REUTZEL, D.R., 7

RICHGELS, D.J., 42

RIMES, 44–45

RISK FACTORS, 56–57

ROLLER, C., 62, 76

ROTHSTEIN, R., 4–5

ROUND-ROBIN APPROACH, 68

ROUTMAN, R., 1

RUNNING RECORDS, 68

RUSSIAN CHILDREN, 22

S

SAGE PROGRAM (WISCONSIN), 15

ST. PIERRE, R.G., 50

SCHOOL CHARACTERISTICS: and achievement, 15–16; and literacy promotion, 35

SCHUSTER, B.V., 42

SCOPE-AND-SEQUENCE APPROACH, 49

SCOTT, J.A., 30–39, 41, 60, 66, 83

SCREENING, 57

SECOND LANGUAGE LEARNERS. *See* students, non–english-speaking

SEIDENBERG, M., 39

SELF-CORRECTION: development of, 59; need for, 33

SELF-DISCOVERY, 49

SELF-MONITORING: development of, 59; need for, 33

SHANAHAN, T., 42

SHARED-BOOK EXPERIENCE, 6

SHORT VOWELS, 45

SHOWERS, B., 14

SLAVIN, R.E., 77

SMITH, F., 34

SNOW, C.E., 5, 14, 17, 18, 21, 23, 27, 52–60, 61

SOFTWARE: for phonemic awareness, 65, 72; for vocabulary instruction, 72

SPELLING: and phonics generalizations, 45, 49

SPELLING PATTERNS: in reading instruction, 3; for writing, 55

SPELLING SKILLS: effect of phonics instruction on, 28

SPIEGEL, D.L., 4, 7, 80

SPUTNIK, 11

SSR. *See* sustained silent reading

STAFF DEVELOPMENT: and achievement, 14–15; coaching in, 14–15; critical areas of, 71; demonstration in, 14–15; and improved reading instruction, 70–71, 74; in phonics instruction, 25; practice in, 14–15; successful models for, 14–15; theory in, 14–15

STAHL, S.A., 39

STAR PROGRAM (TENNESSEE), 15

STEBBINS, L.B., 50

STRICKLAND, D.S., 1, 5, 21, 28, 49–50, 59

STUDENTS: change in thinking about readiness of, 19; characteristics of, 13; expectations of, 52; interest in phonics, 29; Russian, 22

STUDENTS, LOW-INCOME: and phonics instruction, 24, 27; reading aloud to, 46; recommendations for, 57–58; risk factors for, 56–57

STUDENTS, LOW-PERFORMING, 24, 66

STUDENTS, MINORITY: failed programs for, 50; lack of achievement of, 37; and literature, 26; NAEP results for, 58; phonics instruction for, 26; recommendations for, 57–58; research on, 82; risk factors for, 56–57

STUDENTS, NON–ENGLISH-SPEAKING: lack of achievement of, 37; recommendations for, 57; research on, 50–51, 82

SUSTAINED SILENT READING (SSR), 67

SYNTHETIC PHONICS APPROACH, 3, 32

T–U

TAXONOMY OF EDUCATIONAL OBJECTIVES: PART I, COGNITIVE DOMAIN (BLOOM), 23

TEACHER ACTIVITIES, 83–86

TEACHER EDUCATION: and achievement, 14–15; coaching in, 14–15; critical areas of, 71; demonstration in, 14–15; and improved reading instruction, 70–71, 74; in phonics instruction, 25; practice in, 14–15; theory in, 14–15

TEACHERS: characteristics of, 13; exploration of research by, 2; as observers of children's reading ability, 6–7; as researchers, 14–15; support for balanced reading approach from, 1

TECHNOLOGY: and balanced reading approach, 48; effects on student expectations, 52; and improved reading instruction, 71–72; for phonemic awareness, 65, 72; research in, 71–72; for vocabulary instruction, 69

TEMPORARY SPELLING, 45

TEXT STRUCTURE, 31

TEXTS. *See* basal readers; literature

THEORIES, 14–15

TOMPKINS, G.E., 34, 40

TRACEY, D.H., 36

TRANSACTIONAL GROUPS, 67

UNITED KINGDOM, 27

U.S. DEPARTMENT OF EDUCATION, 52

V

VIETNAM WAR, 12

VOCABULARY: controlled, 20, 33; practice of, 43; relationship to reading comprehension, 73

VOCABULARY INSTRUCTION: effect on reading comprehension, 69; methods of, 69; software for, 72

VOWELS, 45

VYGOTSKY, L.S., 6

W

WATERFORD EARLY READING PROGRAM (SOFTWARE PROGRAM), 72

WENRICH, J.K., 8

WHARTON-MCDONALD, R., 7

WHOLE LANGUAGE: basis of, 39; in California educational system, 40; peak of, 1; phonics in, 39

WHY JOHNNY CAN'T READ (FLESCH), 11, 22

WILKINSON, I.A.G., 30–39, 41, 60, 66, 83

WILLIS, I.W., 12, 79, 82

WILLOWS, D.M., 42

Woo, D.G., 36

WORKBOOK PAGES, 34

WRITING: need for, 33; process approach for, 33; spelling patterns for, 55

WRITING TO READ (SOFTWARE PROGRAM), 72

Y

YAGHOUB-ZADEH, Z., 42

YATVIN, J., 74

YOKOI, L., 7